Soul Connection

Relating beyond the surface

Tammy Smith, Ph.D.

ISBN 978-0-9777926-4-1

Unless otherwise noted, Scripture quotations are from the Holy Bible: New International Version. Copyright 1973, 1978, 1984 by International Bible Society.

Printed in the United States of America
Akron, Ohio

To order additional copies of this resource:
ONLINE at www.drtammysmith.com
MAIL Threshold Counseling, 1115 Bethel Rd., Col., OH 43220
FAX order to (614) 451-3017

FOR

Mike – my rock

Shay – my heart

Spence – my joy

Jesus – my everything

ACKNOWLEDGEMENTS

To those who have had a visible hand in this work:

Carol Y. – Your faithfulness to God is evident in every aspect of your life. I continue to be overwhelmed and deeply blessed by your true kinship in matters of the heart and kingdom. You pour yourself out in devotion to Jesus, and such excellence has been foundational to this book. I admire your quiet dedication and true humility. I am blessed by your abiding friendship.

Jen M. – Your partnership in this work has been profound! You have stepped up in every way imaginable and then some. You are a sincere colaborer in the Lord, beautiful friend and sacrificial servant. More significant is how your life embodies the true healing of Christ's life, rising up within to conquer that which sought to destroy you. I couldn't be any more proud of you.

Wendy M. – Even with new life circumstances, you gave of yourself to this book. Your sincere kindness and loyal friendship have continued to be a joy to me. Thank you for being willing to do tiresome research, and always offering encouragement and support just when I needed it.

Mom – What joy to have you on this ride! I am so proud of you and thankful for all your work. You taught me how to work hard at something until it is done, even through obstacles. I am so blessed to have you as my mom. Your love and support mean the world to me.

Kim W. – I cannot express the depth of gratitude I have for your faithful presence in my life. You are so humble, so gifted, and so open to God. Your dedication to His work through these "Soul" ministries has spurred me on towards the God who gave me this treasure in you.

Mike - I thank God for the gift of you every day. You are hilarious, wise, faithful, kind-hearted, principled, and a man of integrity. Your support through this process and especially in this past year has revealed only more what incredible character you have. I love you.

CONTENTS

Introduction
LOOKING WITHIN

Don't people drive you crazy? Really, more than anything else, people can make us crazy—with love, crazy with rage, crazily obsessed, crazily blessed, or just plain out of our minds! Our relationships and interactions with others are often the reasons we can't sleep, can't eat, overeat, under focus, overprotect, get mad, get happy, get depressed, you name it. Because they are dynamic, ever-changing entities, we can't ever completely predict what another person will say or do. Since the human brain is vast in its complexity, combined with the fact that there are no two people exactly alike, we can never entirely know another person. These facts are what compel us to pursue other people, while simultaneously being what cause us to be confounded by them. As a result, our relationships with people can be the place of greatest happiness and love in our lives, as well as being the places in which we experience the most intense pain.

Scripture says, "It is good and pleasant when God's people live together in peace!" (Psalm 133:1). Nothing will bring you more earthly joy than being in God-focused, loving relationships with other humans. We were made for it. However, the challenges along the way for two people to relate with grace, maturity, love, and wisdom can sometimes be so hard, that we just want to give up.

Maybe that's why you've picked up this book.

Perhaps it was an unknown impulse that caused you to open these pages. Maybe your marriage is in a crisis or family in division. Possibly a coworker has you pulling out your hair or you can't seem to get through to your children. Whatever the case, *something* moved you to want to explore this topic. I am so proud of you for following the prompting! You have just established yourself as a strong and wise person. Only above-average people search for tools to better relationships. Now, if you can ignore society's messages to wish for a magic pill, an easy fix, or 10-steps-to-a-miraculously-quick solution, you will get very far indeed.

Our relationships will never change if we don't have a long-term perspective. The very nature of relating implies something that occurs over time and with effort. It's also a fact that we won't enjoy soul connection if we are too busy being focused on how the other person needs to change. Many of us think our relationships would be so much better if only those around us could see what they need to do differently! We subtly believe we make fantastic holy spirits for those closest to us. The fact that you are still reading shows that you understand the all-important reality that it takes two to make a great relationship, just like it takes two to make a bad one. If you are enjoying a nice connection with someone, you are to get part of the credit. If you have a really messed-up relationship right now, you are partly to blame. Because of this, I already want to say "thank you" for being willing to look in the mirror. I'm excited that you are bold enough to admit your relationships really do need help, that you have the power to do something about them, and that there's more for you as a new creation in Christ than settling for the "same old, same old."

Consciously or unconsciously, each one of us is trying to have real and satisfying relationships with others. That's why a bottle can become a best friend, a cupcake a confidant, or an air-brushed image your favorite companion to visit. Some may think they have given it up or grown beyond it, but the truth is that to know and be known is a longing from which we can't escape. This truth, gone awry, is...

- ≈ why a well-liked political leader can trade years of careful posturing for a one-night stand.

- ≈ why people stand up when a hockey brawl ensues (or we are intrigued when people fight).

- ≈ why a national Christian leader will risk a lifetime of shame over a momentary encounter.

- ≈ why reality TV shows are the #1 type of program watched.

- ≈ why people text and chat and blog endlessly.

- ≈ why pornography is pandemic, society is sex-saturated, and millions are spent pitifully on 900 phone numbers.

- ≈ why people practically get giddy when reading the results of spot-on personality tests.

In myriad legitimate and illegitimate ways, human beings are constantly, relentlessly, insatiably being driven by an inner need to be connected to other humans.

We can't help it

Think about it – we actually come from each other. We literally give physical life to each other through an amazing design of the Lord. Why, then, do we miss the fact that this act of giving life is meant to continue throughout our time on earth? The picture of emotionally deprived babies gives us a stark dose of reality. Studies show that infants given love and care thrive while those destitute of attention will wither away, even if offered food and drink.[1] All babies track loved ones through their senses – their eyes follow mom and dad, not random strangers. Their ears are attuned to the voices of familiar people, and they have anxiety when around strangers. You and I were once babies, and the desire to be attached closely to loved ones didn't go away as we matured. It simply took on a different form.

Why else would one of people's greatest fears be dying alone? When it comes to people drawing near their last breaths or hearing news of a sudden life-threatening disease, their racing thoughts go towards relationships. Good-byes, reconciliations, and words of appreciation...no one wants to die feeling like he failed at connecting with others. Even those who spend their lives amassing a fortune admit that money leaves one empty and that relationships are more impor-tant. Similarly, the fact that humans need soul connection is why things were so dramatically different during the days immediately following the 9/11 tragedy. People were kind, sacrificial, patient, engaged, emotional and concerned. Why? Because death came near to all of us that day. Anytime fatality threatens, we automatically think in terms of relationships and the importance of people in our lives. People on the higher floors of the Twin Towers called and left messages with those they held most dear. Similarly, soldiers in war write letters to loved ones to be delivered in case of death.

This is all back-door proof that shows us we were meant to connect. That we *want* to. Likewise, the fact that we were designed for deep relationship is also proven by the reality that nothing else upsets us as much as other humans. Only humans make us furious, comforted, or hurt. Other people get the majority of our thought time. We can easily be found obsessing over the latest thing someone said to us, fretting over how our boss will answer our request, or interpreting whether a "lost" invitation was a relational slight or not. *People* consume most of our internal energy.

In the writing of this introduction, a relative of mine hurt my feelings. Everything in me wanted to pull away, close up, and begin the methodical process of taking back all the vulnerability and heart I've given over the years. Of course, the conversation replayed in my mind, and tears stung the corners of my eyes, at the ready if I should beckon. Why? Because I'm oversensitive? Not generally. Because I've completely misunderstood an innocuous interaction? No. The bottom line for me and for you every time you've felt the hurt of a disrupted interaction is this…relationships matter. Our relationships matter…a lot. Nothing can make us feel worse because nothing on earth matters as much as our connection to other people.

Do you know that most people feel lonely in a crowd? A client of mine said last week, "I want to be a part of people without any pretense. I just want to belong." This underlying need explains how upstanding leaders can trade it all for a night of passion, or a promising genius can trash his life in an addiction. In order to belong to someone or some group, we'll actually do almost anything for those few moments of counterfeit connection. I'm sitting on an airplane as I write, and just about every relational posture known to man is observable in this human Petri dish. I see myriad attempts at engagement all around me. From the freckled Nintendo player to the scantily clad tanning salon operator, no matter what he looks like or how she appears at the moment, each one of them has a need. Whether the overly talkative cowboy or the aloof professor knows it or not, they both crave the same thing. What do you think would happen if the plane started going down? This universal need would be exposed. People would grasp each other, maybe confess, and perhaps weep together. Every human is created with an incontrovertible need for connection with others.

This is why many couples will go to bed tonight depressed after watching a few hours of TV in parallel positions. No turning towards each other. No message that "you are more interesting to me than the latest crime scene show." Similarly, a sense deep inside signals to us that there's something just not right about sending an email to a person in the next cubicle or texting someone in the same room. It's true that we can live for years in relationship with others and not really know them. Even the most resistant to these concepts cannot deny that individuals flourish when they feel loved and cared for by others. People's faces become flush when someone gives them a compliment. Why? Because it taps into this empty reservoir of hopefulness. In other words, it feels really good to be known! Being loved and received is the primary need we have, whether we know it or not.

Your response to the introduction of this book is likely one of two: you totally "get" what is being discussed or you don't (and it sounds like some sort of West Coast indulgence). We can probably find ourselves in one of three categories in this regard: (1) relational funk, (2) relational fear, or (3) relational fog. To be in a "relational funk" is to know and agree with the premise of this book, but to simply be stuck instead of moving your connections with others beyond the superficial. Those in the "relational fear" category know something is missing, but are too afraid to do anything about it. Previous wounds have left them skittish at best or paralyzed at worst.

Those of you who don't really "get" what is being said are also ones who don't know what you're missing relationally. You would be in the third category of "relational fog." For whatever reason, your inner drive and desire to be in quality relationships with others has gone way underground and is not in your active awareness at present. For all three types, I say, "Read on!" There's something for you in these pages. God didn't leave us on this earth with all these other humans, void of any how-tos! My desire for every reader is simple. First, I want you to know that you CAN have relationships that "get there" for you and meet some of those deeper needs. Second, pursuing soul connection is worth it for your good and God's glory. Third, aided by the ever-practical Word of God and fueled by the Spirit, we can acquire some tools for real and lasting change.

Longing understood

We can't move ahead in the work of relationships until we truly understand the "why" of relationships. To relate, to need each other, is to be created in the image of God. God Himself is relational in His very nature. Think about it. He is a Trinitarian being. The Father, Son, and Holy Spirit are constantly working as one, intricately and intimately. God is relational in His essence. It follows that our entire existence is based on relationship. We are conceived through a relational act. We are carried inside another human being until we are birthed, not in some separate vessel like an egg. After birth, our first food is milk created by a human's body. While this picture can be unnerving, it is more disturbing how far we run from our fundamental interdependence as we grow into independence. People keep trying harder and harder to live like they don't need others. Houses now have fences around yards of nine square feet. Eye contact is a lost art. Garage door openers keep some neighbors from ever seeing each other. But, our very genesis demonstrates that we are relational in our DNA.

Call Him Father, call Him brother

We were created by God first and foremost to relate with Him. He invites us to call him Daddy, tells us that Jesus is closer than a brother, and the Holy Spirit actually comes and takes up residence in us if we've called on Christ for salvation (Romans 8:15, 16; Ephesians 1:13). We are adopted as His children (Galatians 3:26, Ephesians 1:5). He invites us to come to Him when we are weary, provides strength when we are weak, and gives peace when we bring every type of prayer to Him (Matthew 11:28, Isaiah 41:10, Philippians 4:6, 7). These are outworkings of a relationship – an ongoing interaction of needing and reaching and connecting. God's design is for us to walk out our days on earth in an intimate and growing relational dependence upon Him.

God's design also establishes that we were meant to live out our days in relationship with others. Your soul, having been made in the image of God, is meant to be connected to others. Human connection is truly God's idea. The second human being was actually created *from* a part of the first! Talk about the picture of connectedness. Some of the earliest recorded words of God include this defining phrase: "It is not good for man to be alone" (Genesis 2:18). You see, the impetus for creating a second human came from this truth which continues to drive us to this day – being alone is not a good idea for God's created ones.

So, not only is the Word clear that we were made to have soul connectedness with God and others, it is also clear on another point: when we are enjoying true relationship with others, God is glorified (1 John 3:18, 19). God is honored and exalted when we relate to each other in true soul connection. Therefore, the ultimate "why" behind striving toward true soul connection for Christians is that God is glorified in our relationships when they reflect Him. How we love, honor, cherish and appreciate God's people is a yardstick for how our life glorifies God. To relate this way reflects God. Jesus summarizes the greatest commandments as "love the Lord your God with all your heart, mind, soul and strength and love your neighbor as yourself" (Matthew 22: 37-39). Relating to others in love is God's idea for us, and as we do it, He gets glory through it.

Larry Crabb and Dan Allender sum up this fact beautifully. They say:

> "God intends that his influence be felt most forcefully through a company of men and women who relate to each other the way God relates. That is where he has chosen to reveal himself,

to make known his relational nature...the divine character, in all its fullness (but especially its gracious love) is meant to be on display among those who participate in the divine nature."[2]

The ever-wise Solomon also states the reality of our need for connection. In Ecclesiastes four, he records, "Two are better than one because they have a good return for their work. If one falls down, his friend can help him up. But pity the man who falls and has no one to help him up! Also, if two lie down together, they will keep warm. But how can one keep warm alone? Though one may be overpowered, two can defend themselves. A cord of three strands is not quickly broken" (verses 9-12). Here, we see the essential benefits of quality relationships are mutual effort, mutual support, mutual encouragement, and mutual strength. Isn't that what we so want?

We also see that Solomon said, "Woe to the one who falls when there is not another to lift him up" (NASV).[3] Woe – sadness, despair, misery, anguish – to the lonely one, indeed. It is not good for God's created ones to be alone. But instead of entering authentically into relationships to bless and be blessed, most people allow fear to deprive them of true fellowship. That is why it has been said, "Few people alive today, at least in western culture, have had a real taste of the power of God through community."[4] The strength in community is the power of connection, a power that enters someone's life with the energy of Christ, to view another with the mind of Christ, and to touch souls with the love of Christ.

Our need for others cannot be underestimated. From the secularist who realizes that "no man is an island" to the Christian who understands that other believers are brothers and sisters in Christ, everywhere we turn we are confronted with this truth. Believers, in particular, are meant for deep interaction with one another, because we are actually considered as members of Christ's body. We are analogously spoken of as various body parts, like toes or kidneys (see 1 Corinthians 12). Our necessary interdependence is undeniable as we look at the Word of God for relational cues.

A proportional relationship

A close read of the Bible shows another interesting dynamic concerning our relationships with others. It is that these relationships are actually an overflow of our relationship with Christ. John says,

> "We love because He first loved us. If anyone says, "I love God," yet hates his brother, he is a liar. For anyone who does not love his brother, whom he has seen, cannot love God, whom he has not seen. And he has given us this command: whoever loves God must also love his brother."
> (1 John 4:19-21)

Could this imply that our worst human relationship will determine the quality of our relationship with God, according to John? At a bare minimum, in human relationships we can most clearly see our deepest struggles with God. The Word says it's just not possible to say, "I love God," and love no other human being (1 John 4:20). If you need a physical representation of your love for an unseen God, then look at the world and see what your heart for God looks like. God's got a heart for people. The bottom line here is that our heart direction toward human beings will reveal what our heart truly believes about God.

If you love God, you're going to love people. Plain and simple. If you don't love your brother, you don't love God. The proportionality of this relationship is seen in the following verse as well: "This is how we know that we love the children of God: by loving God and carrying out his commands" (1 John 5:2). So, as Christians, we cannot deny our need for relationships with others if we truly love God. Further, the Bible assumes that change in our relationship with God will occur in direct proportion to our change in relationships with others. Our relationship with God grows when we move to bless others. The more we love others, the more we will know about the heart of God (John 15:10-14). Because we are His "dearly loved children," He urges us to imitate Himself in the ways we relate to others (Ephesians 5:1). That is, imitate Him in love, for God is entirely loving (1 John 4:8).

Life's measuring stick

If we haven't gotten the picture by now, in terms of our own inherent desires and God's desire for us, the need to be connected to others is a huge measure of our love for Christ and the apparent presence of His Spirit within us. Simply put, the quality of our relationships is the truest measure of our lives. If we honestly sift through the stuff of life, I think we'd all agree that the substance of our relationships -- with God and people -- is the truest gauge of the quality of our lives. When life is weighed in the balance, our relationships of love have far more weight than anything else we can put on the scales. They are our most valued treasures and well worth the time we must invest in them. Their preeminence seems apparent, but often gets lost in the day-to-day grind. Really, have you looked anyone square in the eye yet today? Hugged anyone? Spoken love to someone you love? Or have you been busily getting ready, getting there, or getting done? At the end of our time on earth, we'll never wish we had spent more time at the office or on accomplishments. We will likely, though, wish we had been kinder or gentler to our kids, spouse, parents or friends.

Therefore, take time right now to think of your best relationship and your worst one. Which friend, companion, or family member do you consider the closest, safest, kindest? With whom do you feel most comfortable sharing yourself, leaning on, laughing with? Write the initials of his or her name down somewhere on this page or in a journal or notebook. Now think about your worst relationship. Who is it that you continually struggle with, with whom can you never seem to find an amicable arrangement, or whose very existence is an irritant? Record those initials as well. Turn this book over, and for a few moments think about *why* the best relationship is the best and the worst is the worst. Ponder the components or the misfiring of those connections. Revisiting these two relationships throughout the pages of this book will be a helpful exercise and will, I pray, bring healing to the challenging one, as well as cause you to rejoice in the one that is good.

A hopeful vision

While the hope for better, more fulfilling, and God-honoring relationships is real and attainable, it is also difficult. True soul connection takes effort because it is challenged. The powers of hell will quite literally try to thwart these God-honoring relationships in every way possible. I actually just finished a phone call with a sweet, committed Christian. She told me her roommate asked her to move out. These were best Christian friends, the kind that dreamed of a long life of ministry together – missionary work, living outside the norm, following the example of the early church recorded in Acts. They went into their living arrangement with such excitement, telling all their friends, and were optimistic about how they would be able to encourage and sharpen each other, like God's Word exhorts. And now, just months later, it's all down the drain?! How does this happen? Why? Why, Lord?!? Evil doesn't want you and me, who house the Holy Spirit, to get into true communion. That's because the Word says when we come together in His name, He is right there among us (Matthew 18:20). When that happens, God's Kingdom moves forcefully. Therefore, to move toward true soul connection is to realize two very important truths: First, your soul longs for and was created for deep relationships with others. Second, those very relationships will be pelted with hellish arrows to keep them from succeeding.

You have your hands on a dangerous weapon. Applying the Lord's principles for relationships can change your life, even to the point of having a massive impact on the people around you. Your soul longs for honest, sincere, knowing, caring connection because you were created in the image of a relational God whose idea it was for us to relate closely in the first place! You are not alone. In actuality, if most people were honest, they'd tell you they're longing for more in their interactions with others. So, by faith as you move forward in this book, some of what you read will be relational basics whereas other sections explain interactive subtleties. God has given us His Word as our handbook for life, so let us glean all we can from His example and teachings and watch them change our connections with others. I guarantee (yes, a money-back one!) that something in this book will apply to you, enlighten you, and afford you an opportunity to see the life of Christ more manifest in your relationships.

Chapter One
LOOK BEYOND

Jesus provides us many strong pictures for true relating. The Word of God contains reference upon reference for how to treat one another, honor one another, love one another, and so on. There is an overall posture towards others that is clearly discernible through multiple passages of Scripture. It is captured in "Love each other deeply, because love covers over a multitude of sins," and "You, then, why do you judge your brother?" (1 Peter 4:8, Romans 14:10). The sense being conveyed here seems to be a "look beyond" capacity. In a society where many jobs are given based upon external appearances, assessments are made on first impressions, and decisions about future interactions are made upon initial conversations, the temptation is to base much of what we think about others on how we judge them from the outside. This is completely contrary to Jesus' way of approaching others.

He invited beggars to banquets, prostitutes to prayer meetings, and tax collectors to the table. Jesus embodied what Samuel described: "…man looks at the outward appearance, but God looks at the heart" (1 Samuel 16:7). His determination to focus on the heart of a person was remarkable. Instead of seeing an abrasive, impulsive loud-mouth, Jesus saw in Peter true leadership and passion. When others saw an adulteress,

Jesus saw a tender heart needing release from condemnation. While Jews wouldn't even associate with Samaritans, Jesus engaged in intellectual dialogue with a woman of a storied past. To Jesus, the woman who reached out to touch His cloak was not a pushy beggar, but a determined believer. A shady tax collector was, to Him, a dogged seeker.[5] The woman who poured a year's worth of wages in perfume on His feet was not a wasteful show-off, but a true worshipper.[6] At my core, I thank Him that He sees us with those same eyes today – eyes full of grace, mercy, and forgiveness.

Resolutely choose to stare at the heart of a person.

If we are to not only be His disciples, but also to pursue deep connection with others, we must likewise develop the capacity to "look beyond." *To do this is simply to be determined that, no matter what the external presentation is in any form, you will resolutely choose to stare at the heart of a person.* It is to intentionally *see further* than what the five senses can apprehend. If someone is beautiful, you will no more give him credibility in your mind than if he is deformed. If a person presents herself as aloof, you will not walk away, but instead pursue her just as you would any other. Whether a man seems cocky, intelligent, effeminate, overbearing, insecure, capable or charming, you continue interested and loving interactions, no matter what. If a woman looks like a model or a maid, has the personality of a sweetheart or a sourpuss, or seems to be confident or coy – whatever her outward appearance – you don't "bite." Instead, you look beyond the external, her personality, and apparent appearance until you can get a sense of what her heart is. It's following the example of Jesus.

Bring on the grace

To "look beyond" is, most simply put, extending the grace of God to others. The beautiful words in 1 Peter 4:10 remind us that this is our calling: "Each one should use whatever gift he has received to serve others, faithfully administering God's grace in its various forms." We are to faithfully administer God's grace. Because "administer" is a dubious word for us, I looked up the definition for clarity. Its various meanings include: be in charge of, dispense, give as medication, perform as ritual, look after somebody.[7] What a phenomenal picture for us! You are in charge of giving out God's grace...to dispense it...to give God's grace out like medication...to give God's grace out so often as to be ritual-like about it...to look after someone gracefully! Indeed, God's grace is quite aptly depicted as a healing agent. To "look beyond" will undoubtedly have a life-saving effect on some of the people you encounter.

This extension of God's grace to others can be captured by having the attitude, "I am what I am by the grace of God. I let you be what you are by the grace of God." Said differently, "God extended His riches at Christ's expense for me, so I can certainly give you my best thoughts, wishes, and kindness."[8] Exercising grace means we believe that others who look completely different from us can be just as or more spiritual. A good way to assess the grace you are (or are not) extending is by asking yourself about conversations and interactions you have with others:

≈ "Did I extend grace or add to their guilt feelings?"

≈ "Am I encouraging their freedom and victory in Christ or not?"

≈ "Am I judging or accepting?"

≈ "Do I feel like I know better than they do, or am I open to their perspectives?"

Hebrews 12:15 tells us plainly: "See to it that no one misses the grace of God and that no bitter root grows up to cause trouble and defile many." We are indeed to see to it that God's grace is our marching order. In this way, we will most accurately reflect the life of Christ in our own. Instead of alienating people from the gospel through caustic judgmentalism or Bible-thumping condemnation, we will draw them closer to the One who lives within us...by His grace alone.

Blinded by the facade

I'll never forget how the Lord seared the "you must look beyond" message on my heart, never to be forgotten. In the early years of ministry, I led a youth group for awhile. One group of students who came in as 7th graders were seniors by the time Mike and I discovered we would be moving. That class contained many students who had been with me the entire course of their high school years. It was a complete privilege to watch many of them grow in the Lord and make their faith their own. One student, though, never seemed to want to be there. Ever. In all those years, whenever addressed, Daniel would shrug his shoulders, say "I don't know," or make some smart-aleck response. He didn't close his eyes to pray, fell asleep during talks, and looked like he hated every minute of being there. The curious thing was that he was always there. We concluded his parents must have made him attend.

At the end of every gathering time, I would stand at the door and hug every student. It was my tradition, and even first-timers were jokingly told by regular attendees that it was a requirement to get out the door. Daniel would routinely try to dodge me or sneak out the back. When I did hug him, he gave me the lifeless rag response, from the time he was a scrawny 7th grader to a 250-pound senior. But, lurk he would, until I found him and got my hands around his adolescent self. He would take it, and then get out like lightning.

So, when it came time for us to leave, the students threw a wonderful good-bye celebration for us. It included encircling all the students who then went around and one-by-one shared their heartfelt thanks and farewells. Because we had been with many of these kids for so many years, it was quite emotional and beautiful. Some of them found words beyond their years. Then came Daniel's turn. Of course, as all eyes turned to him, he made no eye contact. In typical, but still awkward, silence from him, we sat. Then, he dropped his head, buried it in his hands, and made dramatic crying noises. Students shifted uncomfortably and others giggled, thinking it was just another of Daniel's shenanigans. His best friend, seated beside him, looked at me apologetically.

So, to break the ice and call his bluff, I said, "Oh, Daniel, are you *c-r-ying*?" Even as I type this, I am sickened, because he was! Daniel was actually crying! He wasn't joking, and it didn't stop. He cried and cried, as his brother who sat across the circle looked at everyone with a wide-eyed "I've-never-seen-him-do-this-before" look. Before long, he was sobbing. His best friend stared at him in total shock, and I believe at that point Daniel muttered some words about us not leaving because he didn't want us to...I don't know because I didn't really hear his words. I only heard my own regret pounding through my soul – that I bought into his external presentation. Yes, for six years it was consistent. Yes, there seemed to be no crack in the shell. No excuse. If we love Christ, we must follow His example to believe more about people than what we can see. We must be resolute in our determination to look beyond and stare at the hearts of others – to their wounds, their fears, their joys, their secret hopes. Daniel burned this message on my soul. Humans look at outward appearance, but God stares at the heart. If we have claimed Christ as our own, God lives in us by His Spirit, and *He* will refocus us to the hearts of others if we will let Him live His life in us.

The lesson that Daniel taught me was that one can never know entirely what another person is thinking or feeling by looking at him from the outside. In my office, I have been blessed to work with millionaires, students, politicians, housewives, pastors, doctors, and athletes. Unequivocally, I know now we can never judge the inside from viewing the outside. Even when it might seem from all outward indications that a person clearly feels one way, he or she could in actuality be feeling quite the opposite. Have you ever seen anyone laugh at a horribly inappropriate time, like when someone else starts crying or gets hurt? The one laughing is certainly not amused. Have you seen someone crying only to quickly discover they're not sad, but super angry? How about the person who shuts down in seemingly angry silence only to find out her feelings were so hurt, she was trying to keep from crying? How often has someone said to you, "Are you okay?" when you were just deep in thought? We've got to get it in our heads that we can't judge from the outside.

Spiritual x-ray vision

Just like Jesus, we have to refuse to be deterred or enticed by outward presentation. Prostitute, preacher, and pre-schooler should all get the same treatment from us. In love, we have to look through people's words and their actions to see God's creation in them. The apostle Paul said that those "who seemed to be important" didn't get any special attention from him because "God does not judge by external appearance" (Galatians 2:6). To "look beyond" is a solemn determination to get to a person's heart and see beyond exteriors.

An old Ray Boltz song captures the sentiment, "When others see a shepherd boy, God may see a king."[9] One of my son's teachers recently spoke these words about him to indicate that we cannot see today who a child will be in the future. Such a posture towards everyone we know will beget the skill of "looking beyond." I cannot begin to capture what impact you will have on others if you can become someone committed to this attitude. To look beyond is to offer others hope, free them from labels, and validate them as individuals. I've always said junior high workers have been bestowed with this ability naturally, but the rest of us must work at it. It involves a resolve to "recognize no man according to the flesh" as is recorded in 1 Corinthians 5:16. Often we identify ourselves and each other primarily by what we look like (tall, short, fat, skinny) or what we do (accountant, carpenter, nurse, engineer). However, looking beyond doesn't allow us to settle into such a routine.

Especially as it relates to Christians, we must look beyond, because we know for certain there is something better within! Do you follow me? If someone has accepted Christ's sacrifice on his behalf and now claims Him as Lord, that means the Spirit of Christ Himself dwells within him! Certainly, it is worth looking beyond human irritations with these brothers and sisters. That's why as Christians, when we are asked to identify ourselves in relation to our faith, we must stray away from sharing our role in the church or what we are *doing* for the Lord. That's just walking into the world's trap. We must see ourselves and others in the faith as much, much more than any descriptor, job title, or personality characteristic. We are all fearfully and wonderfully made workmanships of God Himself, whose righteousness has been imputed to us (Psalm 139:14, Ephesians 2:10, 2 Corinthians 5:21). That's how we are to view one another.

Mike and I had friends in our first church whose marriage was intriguing to all who knew them. It was fascinating to behold, because they were complete opposites -- he being of Harley-bike-rider ilk and she a prototypical elementary school teacher. Many people wondered how they got together, stayed married, and even interacted on a day-to-day basis. When we got up the nerve, after years of knowing them, to ask how they worked so well despite radical differences, they looked at each other and matter-of-factly said, "Well, we recognize that the other person is 100% righteous because of Christ, so we choose to actually view each other as perfect." They were radical in practicing the point of 2 Corinthians 5:21: "God made him who had no sin to be sin for us, so that in him we might become the righteousness of God." To their credit, they were extreme about taking God at His Word, each believing that the other was fully righteous in Christ. Therefore, for them to focus on the other's imperfections was an affront to God. To complain about their perfect spouse was to profane a work of Christ. They totally chose to focus on the 100% righteousness of Christ in the other person as opposed to the equally as real 100% flesh that we are all still trapped in this side of heaven. This complexity is a derivative of the already/not yet reality of God's Kingdom. God's victory is already completed in its entirety, but not yet fully realized.

The severe aim of my friends serves as a beautiful example of what it means to "look beyond."

Eyes of compassion

One clear tactic the Lord has given me to help keep my gaze off outward presentation is to imagine that emotional wounds are as visible as physical ones. Literally try to picture a parallel physical wound for emotional ones, like a missing limb for sexual abuse, being wheelchair bound for death of parents, or a physical scar for a friend's betrayal. I have spoken of this at conferences and elsewhere, and have seen it be a seriously transformative perspective for people. No one gets to adulthood without some measure of emotional damage. So, attempting to imagine or picture those wounds from a physical viewpoint can help us to look beyond.

Think about the people you know well. Who would you picture with a large scar? Who would be walking around in crutches? Which of your friends might be missing a leg, emotionally-speaking? I truly believe our interactions would be radically different if emotional damage was evident. We'd never expect a hug from an armless person, so why do we get disappointed when a friend whose parents abandoned him can't seem to just trust us for once? Much like our attitude toward the person with a large scar, maybe we wouldn't be so frustrated with a friend's pervasive insecurity. We wouldn't ask our neighbor in a wheelchair to run a marathon with us, so why do we expect of our girlfriend who was beaten to "get beyond" her anxiety? I'm certainly not advocating tolerance, victim-mentality-living or excuses. I believe in Jesus we can fully live beyond past hurts. I'm simply advocating that understanding and compassion can bring radical change to our relationships by allowing us to "look beyond." I fully address the person who is wounded in *Soul Healing* and else-where, but here am advocating Jesus' way – that of focusing on a person's deep character rather than his or her outward functioning.

Tunneling to the core

This perspective of looking beyond enables us to see others and ourselves as we really are: layered. Much like tunneling into the earth, penetrating through one layer only reveals another, significantly different in kind and function. It is very rare when it comes to people that what you see what you get. Remembering this and looking beyond initial layers to behold deeper ones is relational wisdom. Determination to see people through the eyes of Christ often allows us glimpses of an inner core. If, however, you are easily irritated or put off by someone's outer layer, you can often miss out on a fantastic relationship. Think about the times you have had a bad first impression of someone, only to have him or her become a close friend later on in life. Consider the layers you personally have…you are confident in some ways and insecure in others, you have quirks and capabilities, and you have faith and fears. We are wise when we are willing to see others as equally layered, and subsequently stop making one-dimensional judgments of them.

A concrete picture for me of our inner complexity is something I once saw done on television. Studies have focused on the two halves of people's faces and how radically different they can be. Researchers have used computer imaging to isolate one half of a person's face and then produce a mirror image of it. They then fused these two together only to find that the outcome was drastically different from the actual person.[10] Their studies propose multiple conclusions about half-face differentials, but my take-away was that people really are like their faces. They have many "faces" within them, and when we stop at the mere outward presentation at a particular time, we completely fail to capture the real spirit of a person. Being determined to look and listen for deeper meanings and understandings in people is a move enabled by the Spirit, which will always yield a result. It reminds me of Paul's word to "fix our eyes not on what is seen, but on what is unseen. For what is seen is temporary, but what is unseen is eternal" (2 Corinthians 4:18). Oh, that we could focus on God's perspective -- what doesn't meet the eye -- in all areas of our lives, including our spouses, savings accounts, and spiritual battles!

Project in progress

In his letter to the Philippians, Paul gives us a clue to God's perspective on people. He often expressed appreciation and belief in their continued growth. In chapter one verse six, he said, "For I am confident of this, that He who began a good work in you will continue to perfect it until the day of Christ Jesus' return." I used to live in a small town that had many old homes, complete with unique architecture, turrets, and wrap-around porches. Some of these were beautiful, kept in good condition over the years by responsible owners. Others, though, were damaged. Sometimes rundown homes were purchased by people who had a vision to restore them to their original conditions. Imagine that you regularly drove by one of these homes. At first, you would see old paint being scraped off and a section beginning to be redone in rich colors. Next you might see a once-painted-over stained glass window revealed. Your curiosity would likely increase each time you drove by to the point where you looked forward to seeing what changes had happened recently. It is exciting to see something beautiful restored back to its original condition after it has been darkened, damaged, or dilapidated.

This is the precise perspective that Paul clues us to keep toward one another. If we have claimed Christ, God's promise is that He will continue to work in us to change us to Christlikeness as long as we walk this earth. Isn't that exciting? To think that He will never stop molding and remaking us to our intended, restored state is a liberating truth! It means that who I have been in the past is not necessarily who I will be in the future if I let God have His way in my life. In five years, I might actually be more patient or less worrisome or kick this addiction or change that annoying habit. In ten years, lifelong judgmentalism could be gone, mercy could be increased, and contentment might reign in a believer's life. How hopeful a thought! This wonderful truth is not only true for us, but also for our brothers and sisters in Christ.

Therefore, we need to view each other like that house under restoration. With excitement, we need to peer deeply for the next smallest change, to be excited about the fresh paint, redone walls, and reinforced structures. Our ability to see beyond someone's obvious faults to the beautiful deeper work God is doing in them could impact a life deeply. This is Jesus' way. When others would have seen Peter's multiple failings, Jesus saw the strong man he would become (Matthew 16:18).[11] Can you become someone who looks forward to how God is working in another's life? Or have you moved on from someone because she is just too damaged? For us as believers, the promise for continued growth is assured, and all the more if we deliberately and consistently choose to walk in the ways God has clearly laid out. He is in a process of restoring all things, including us, to our intended state, just like those beautiful houses undergoing restoration.[12]

Practically, this means that we are in deep error if we hold fellow Christians to a standard of who they were years ago. In the same way that we ourselves do not want to be seen as the very same person we were five or ten years ago, we must not lock others to a certain stage in their development. Have you cut off a relationship with someone because of an insensitive thing he said to you two years ago? Slowly distanced yourself from a person who let you down? Some family members don't even talk because of a disagreement over some minor issue many years prior. We are wrong to hold others to a standard to which we wouldn't want to be held. Jesus said it plainly, "Do not judge, or you too will be judged. For in the same way you judge others, you will be judged, and with the measure you use, it will be measured you" (Matthew 7:1).

As we ask other believers to give us room to change and grow, do we give them the same chance? Just last night, I sat with a friend whom I haven't seen in 20 years. He told me something I said in college, and not only did I have zero recollection of saying it, I couldn't believe I had. Imagine if he had held on to my immature statement from so long ago and not given me space to have grown in Christ. We can't forget that we are all unfinished people. Just as a house under renovation changes over time, we must excitedly watch to see what Christ forms of Himself in others (Galatians 4:19).

A new prescription

Seeing through a person's external presentation, excitedly looking at him or her as the beautiful home under restoration, and envisioning as physical what level of emotional damage he or she has are all ways to practice the principle of "looking beyond." Another tool in this toolbox is to intentionally attempt to see another through the eyes of Christ. I call it "Christifying." It's as if you don a pair of glasses that gives you Jesus' perspective on others. The religious zealots (teachers of the law and Pharisees) went to stone a woman whom Jesus refused to condemn (John 8). Whereas humans lauded the Pharisees, Jesus called them out for pride and self-promotion. Instead of a tax collector, Jesus saw a seeker. Instead of a seeing a despicable murderer, Jesus saw Saul as a person who needed Him. Who do you see? Someone who is offensive, or probably insecure? Someone who is manipulative, or needing love? Someone who drives you nuts, or has a very different style from who God made you to be? Someone who needs to be the center of attention, or a person wanting affirmation? Someone who is bossy, or someone who is trying to be the person she believes God wants her to be?

As depicted above, to put on the Christ glasses is to essentially don a perspective of grace. Christifying is a deliberate attempt to see people as Christ sees them. If you do this long enough, I have an exclusive and delightful guarantee for you. As you refuse to look at external presentation, as you doggedly attempt to focus on what is unseen and not what meets the eye, and as you stare at the heart of an individual, people actually become more beautiful to you. I'm entirely sincere on this point. When people's souls emerge, they actually look more attractive to you. Because it is a transaction that is spiritual in nature, I can't explain how, but I can tell you that it will happen to you if you practice looking beyond long enough. Let me know how it goes for you!

Problems in the beyond

Interestingly, when you choose to put on these Christ glasses and commit yourself to seeking His perspective on people and things, you will become much more discerning. Discernment is the ability to understand people's layers, motivations, and interactions with tremendous acumen. This can create a quandary. How do discerning people "look beyond" when what they see beyond is clearly problematic? Perhaps only those with deeper discernment understand my point here, so please hang on, dear reader. How does a person with a God-given gift of deep discrimination into human functioning "look beyond"? I found an answer to this question in a thought from Larry Crabb. He inferred that the definition of wisdom is seeing ten things and saying only one.[13] This made so much sense that I have been at peace ever since!

If you have discernment, you can still look beyond as you deal with people. It's just that you have an added responsibility. Oswald Chambers put it this way, "Discernment is God's call to intercession, never to fault finding."[14] You are called to pray about what you see. And if you indeed are to eventually speak about some of what you are sensing, then God will make it clear as you pray. Most likely, this will only occur at Crabb's one-to-ten ratio. Discernment, or the ability to see other's hidden aspects more readily than most, is never a license to judge or condemn. Evaluation is *not* why God gives discernment as we look beyond. Spiritual discernment is given by the Spirit of God and is for mature believers (1 Corinthians 2:14, Hebrews 5:14). Prayer, petition, intercession, care, concern, and love are all appropriate outworkings of discernment. If you are to speak to another about his or her sin, faults, or shortcomings, God will orchestrate that. In the meantime, you pray.

"Here comes the thing"

Our lives are better the minute we can realize that everybody has a "thing." Seriously, everyone has some thing, usually some *big* thing, with which they are dealing. Whether we notice it or not is not the issue. The reality is that people, by virtue of being human beings in a sinful world, struggle. Everyone has issues. We all have quirks, blind spots, sinful patterns, and wounds which make us act in all manner of ways. If it's not his defensiveness or her foul mouth, it will be another's anxiety attacks or all-encompassing insecurity. When your usually pristine Christian boss comes in with a hangover or your pastor uses a colorful expletive when he stubs his toe, what do you do? How do your thoughts go when your Bible study leader gossips? While you can expect it of parents in the stands at your daughter's volleyball game, why are you surprised when the church secretary tells you an off-color joke?

I've personally known millionaires who worry that they're gay, medical doctors who feel inadequate and insecure, mothers of wonderful children who hide out in their homes for fear of rejection, high-level government workers who can't drive their own cars because of panic attacks, and pastors who have been addicted to pornography. *We can't realize this strongly enough or soon enough: all people everywhere have struggles on the inside that will eventually surface.* When it does, how do you respond? Do you gasp in shock? Do you relish the realization that you're not the only sinner around? Do you look forward to being able to tell a friend about it as soon as possible? Or, do you, with humble understanding, continue to interact with this person from a godly, accepting, perspective?

In my mind's eye, whenever I picture someone's "thing" revealing itself, I envision a neon sign above the person's head that says, "Here comes the thing." The understanding that everyone has an issue will help free us from being caught off guard or deeply disappointed when it surfaces. Certainly, I'm not advocating an acceptance of sin or placating or enabling destructive patterns. Instead, I am merely noting that we set ourselves up to be so much more Christlike and mature in our responses

All people have struggles on the inside that will eventually surface.

to people when we are not placing too high of expectations on them. They are not perfect. They are not our saviors. When we realize that even our very favorite people have issues, whether we can yet see them or not, we are in a better position to have true soul connection. Even if I have known someone for awhile and he or she does something I could be offended by, could judge, or could be shocked by, the perspective of "here comes the thing" has enabled me to, with great empathy and compassion, say inside my head, "Oh, there it is. That must be his or her 'thing.' I knew something would surface eventually."

And then? The truest, most godly response to any such discernment is to pray for that person. Prayer for another person staves off judgment. Any insight we gain into how someone truly feels, thinks, or operates should be treated as a precious gift that we offer back to the Lord. "Lord, I can see now that Amy is bitter over her previous church situation. I pray you would enable her to forgive." "Wow, Father. I never thought Silas was stubborn before, but how he acted in that situation showed me it's obviously an area of struggle for him. I pray you would continue to refine him just like you are refining me because of your infinite goodness to us as your created beings."

Just the other day, I heard a sister in Christ who leads multiple Bible studies use a word to describe a bodily function that I wouldn't use in a public setting. Goodness, if my other friend had been there, she probably would have walked out of the room. Does that mean this woman is any less godly? Does that mean we now need to view her differently? How often do we tend to do this when we're up-close-and-personal with people? We have to fight against our propensity to put people on pedestals. As much as we've seen it time and time again, when our favorite star personality gets arrested or divorced, we can't help but feel disappointed. We really do want to believe that there is a way to escape it, to find someone who has it all together.

I've noticed this, having had the privilege of teaching in public contexts with many groups. Whenever people have read a book I've written or heard me speak, they can be excited to interact with me, thinking I am going to converse just like I author or teach God's Word. While I try to be consistent in my person, whether in my home or in front of a group (you may ask my family), I'm still just that -- a *person*. I have insecurities, I need reassurance, I engage in superficial dialogue, I overeat, I speak before thinking, in addition to trying to be prayer-filled, God-centered, Spirit-following, Scripture-minded, and truth-speaking. It's funny, but sometimes people who have only known me from a distance seem a bit disappointed when they realize that I, too, wear this troublesome and ill-fitting garment of humanity this side of heaven. It seems we all have too high expectations of others. For the good of ourselves and others, we need to stop.

We are all unfinished learners this side of heaven. That's what a disciple is – a learner. We are all in the process of becoming what God wants us to be. No one has arrived, and no one ever will in this lifetime. As I type, I am listening to a message left on my voice mail in the middle of last night. The person is talking about being "addicted to people" and how this addiction rules his life. "I make people, everyone, people in general, into my God. I know that. Being with people and being validated by people. I know I have to cry to God, and I do, but I am so sick of this thing." Aren't you so sick of your "thing"? Don't you want others to treat you gently and with respect even when your sin areas are exposed or your struggles revealed? To maturely realize that all people have issues that haunt them is another aspect of learning to "look beyond." It's just another way to look beyond our own perception of someone.

Finally, to acknowledge that everyone in our lives has a "thing" or two affords those of us who are too hard on ourselves the opportunity to back off on this. Instead of spending our days with massive self-hatred for our own issues, realizing that everyone has something can lead to freedom and even relief. In some ways, we might even be able to get to the place of being grateful that that's *all* we have to deal with. "At least I don't have Sasha's cancer or Tony's parents." "Gosh, my wife's and my sex life doesn't seem so bad after realizing that the so-and-so's haven't been able to make love for years." And for those of us who don't really think we have issues at all, think again. If you are brave enough, ask your loved ones what they are. You're sure to have some blind spots revealed then.

As Christ accepted you

To embrace that every person we meet, even our role model or hero in the faith, has issues and struggles that make her seem less than perfect can be a disappointing reality. This realization, though, frees us up to deeper acceptance. As we've already discussed, being able to extend large amounts of acceptance is a sign of true maturity. It also helps us live in more substantial authentic community with others. I'm not accepting just what I observe about you, I am actually accepting of the deeper facets of you I'm coming to know. Such acceptance is a practical outworking of how to extend grace to another.

Romans 15:7 says plainly that we are to accept one another as Christ has accepted us. God is full of grace, placing no requirement upon us. We must liberate others to the same freedom Christ gives us. He accepts us without stipulation. We are not told to clean up our act and then come to Him, but instead He meets us right where we are. "Come near to God and He will come near to you," says James 4:7. "Never will I leave you nor forsake you," He records in Hebrews 13:5. For a holy and completely pure God to commune that intimately with us, He must do a lot of "accepting" of our ridiculously finite ways! God sees beyond my sin through the eyes of Christ to the creation He made in me. Talk about looking beyond.

Oh, how we struggle to accept, though. Truth be told, this is really a challenging topic. Do you accept the tattooed teen whose loud music threatens to introduce you to a hearing aid as you sit at the red light? What about that ethnic group that seems so cocky? Or dirty? Or uneducated? Really, getting down to brass tacks here, it saddens me to admit that in American Christianity, we often limit our acceptance to people who aren't much different from us. Instead, if we could only embody Paul's words in 2 Corinthians: "So from now on we regard no one from a worldly point of view" (verse 5:16).

I'll never forget what happened to a pastor friend of mine. He had a great gift for conversational evangelism, and in his affable way, engaged a motorcycle rider who was taking a break in a parking lot one day. They talked for a bit, and as it was time to go, Doug invited him to church. He told him where it was and what time it started. Doug didn't tell his new friend he was a pastor. The following Sunday at about 10 minutes after the start of the service, there was a loud ruckus in the parking lot. Lo and behold, the motorcyclist and his lady appeared. The lone two-wheeled vehicle around, they simply parked alongside the curb, thus garnering an usher's attention. As they dismounted from the bike and snuffed out their cigarettes under their boots, they looked around until they found an entrance. They entered, clad in various pieces of black leather, both with flowing hair. The congregation was singing a song, and to the discomfort of the ushers who were now exchanging glances, it quickly became obvious that nearly all the seats were full, especially those in the back. So, with his arm draped over his girlfriend, the motorcycle man proceeded to walk down the center aisle towards a pew in the front. Looking around, taking it all in as one would the first time in a new place, he caught a glance of Doug on the stage. Surprised, he exclaimed, "Hey, Doug! How the hell are ya?!"

You play it out in your mind. Were the followers of Christ in the church that day able to look beyond? Who talked to the visitors? What was the conversation like? Did they feel accepted, or was it as obvious to them as it was to everyone else how very different they were? Our acceptance and grace will draw a person to Christ much quicker than our Bible knowledge and standards. Accepting people in grace means we don't put them under any guidelines, even about what being a Christian should look like.

Looking beyond means we don't enter someone's life as judge or critic or even consultant. If we are eager to pounce on sin or correct error, we are certainly not focused on the vision of who he or she is becoming in Christ. Accepting one another as Christ has accepted us makes us question: are there limits to my extension of grace? Do I judge when a friend doesn't take my suggestion? Do I quit calling when a sister has not returned my last few calls? Do I have a subtle list of "I do this, then she does this" rules? Do I notice when I've done something for a friend who hasn't responded with a "thank you"? Am I angered by one who volunteers advice to me, thinking, "I could point out a thing or two about her life!"? Deep acceptance is an aspect of truly looking beyond. In Christ, can I not only look beyond external presentation, but can I also see past minor offenses, misunderstood actions, and differences in personal preference?

Overlooking offense

A final aspect of the choice to look beyond for the sake of soul connection is made plain in Proverbs 19:11. It says, "A man's wisdom gives him patience; it is to his glory to overlook an offense." *Glory to overlook an offense?* Certainly, this captures the heart of "looking beyond." We let go of petty issues, forgive hurtful statements, and give the benefit of the doubt to someone's motive. Why? Because we realize we are to "be kind and compassionate to one another, forgiving each other just as in Christ God forgave you" (Ephesians 4:32). Holding on to grievances and being unforgiving are guaranteed relationship stoppers. The plain truth is that if you are unwilling to allow the Lord to make you a forgiving person, your walk with Him will be stunted and your relationships will be void of any true connection.

The best premarital book Mike and I read was not about the differences between men and women, how to determine roles, or even how to manage conflict. The author who impacted us deeply was one who asserted that marriage boils down to living a lifestyle of forgiveness. When we marry, if we are serious about it, we are committing to ongoing, regularly forgiving each other.[15] Why? Because we're humans! At our core, we are self-seeking sinners who really want things the way we want them. However, to take our relationships to the level of true soul connection, we must become willing to practice steady, consistent forgiveness.

If we are not willing, we are in direct contradiction with the word of God, which tells us to "bear with each other and forgive whatever grievances you may have against one another. Forgive as the Lord forgave you" (Colossians 3:13). The concept of bearing with one another conveys the sense of "over and over and over and over." Generally, we think we're doing well with someone if we've forgiven him once, let alone the seventy times seven Jesus prescribes (Matthew 18:21). His life was a continual expression of the mercy of God, which stands in contrast to our society's demand for compensation from those who injure us. Even as Jesus hung on the cross listening to taunts, he asked his Father to forgive them (Luke 23:34).

The principles of acceptance and forgiveness from Scripture seem to indicate that we will give away the same kind of love, acceptance, and forgiveness that we think we are receiving from God. The Scriptural principle is that "he who is forgiven little, loves little" (Luke 7:47). Conversely, that would imply that he who has been forgiven much forgives much. If you are not aware of just how much God has forgiven you, then most certainly you will struggle with having a continually forgiving spirit. But, if you stay close enough to the Lord through His Word and in times of worship, I am certain you will realize more and more every day the massive, all-encompassing, profound, uncontainable forgiveness we have for past, present, and even future sins because of the Lord Jesus. Only from this stance can we willingly and freely overlook offenses from those around us on a regular basis. With the perspective of His great mercy, we can obey the command to "be merciful, just as your Father is merciful" (Luke 6:36).

It is foolishness or naiveté to spend life trying to avoid being hurt by others. Yet, so many of us spend much time doing whatever we can to protect our feelings. But, it really is impossible! A fact you can bank upon about human beings is that *hurt people hurt people*. Who hasn't been hurt? No one! Therefore, part of life is getting hurt, and by God's design, learning to love through that hurt and look beyond through the prescription of forgiveness. To practice forgiveness daily, as one has learned to brush his or her teeth, is a necessary, rewarding, and freeing aspect of the true Christ-follower's life.

Who do you need to forgive today?

What do you need to overlook/get over today?

His eyes, not yours

We begin a book on soul connection with a chapter on "looking beyond" because we can't connect with others' souls until we can behold them! We can't have deeper relationships with others until we can actually look deeper. If we are too busy assessing, judging, or even reacting to others, then we will never move beyond surface interactions.

The "look beyond" boils down to acceptance and forgiveness. Are you willing to resolvedly stare at the heart of another? Are you willing to accept what you see, no matter how you personally feel about it? Will you become a forgiving soul, freed up from the chains of small-minded bitterness and petty grievances? To begin to view others from such a perspective will cause a chain reaction of dramatic proportion in your own heart and the perspectives of those around you. It is following Paul's example to "regard no one from a worldly point of view" (2 Corinthians 5:16). Donning the name of Christ changes your forever. Donning the eyes of Christ changes your today.

Chapter Two
LOVE BIG

In Ephesians 5:8, we are exhorted to live as children of the light. I believe the phrase that captures the sentiment of this passage is that as children of God we are to "love big". It is as straightforward as it seems; there is no reason to withhold or limit the love that we give others. We must be willing to dole out the love of Christ in large doses. A second meaning to this concept is that we love *like the big person*. In every situation, there is an opportunity to act like a mature, thoughtful, wise adult or to act like a child. Essentially, to love big is to choose the path of being the more giving, less self-protective person in a relationship.

To "love big" is to follow the example of our Lord. Our love for others is usually measured by their degree of cooperation with our plans. If God loved us in this same way, I'm afraid we wouldn't be loved at all! But that's what's amazing about our Lord – He can love us from pure motives with no hidden agenda, never expecting to get anything in return. It is the picture of sacrifice. To lovingly sacrifice for the sake of others is to manifest the life of Christ. To love big involves this type of sacrificial, unconditional approach.

Open your mouth...and bless

One of the easiest ways we can love big is to be encouraging to the people with whom we are in relationship. The power of affirmation can never be overestimated. Mark Twain even said, "I can go for two months on one good compliment."[16] Certainly, everyone can relate to the power of encouraging words. Whether a statement you will never forget from an elementary school teacher, or the compliments you are *not* getting from someone by whom you want to be affirmed, encouraging words impact us all. We long for them, we crave them, we work for them, we relive them after getting them, and we need them.

God's Word is clear that we are to help meet this need in others. In Hebrews 10:24 and 25, we are told to "consider how we may spur one another on toward love and good deeds. Let us not give up meeting together...but let us encourage one another." In the original Greek, "consider" encompasses the ideas of observing and contemplating. The word "encourage" comes from *parakaelo*, which translates to aid, comfort, encourage, exhort, or beseech, and is intended to produce a particular effect.[17] We are to actively perceive and think about how to best encourage each other. Our duty is to do everything in our power to produce the desired effect of another person being encouraged, whether through comforting, exhorting, or simply helping them. Words of belief and honor do indeed help us, give us comfort, and also significantly motivate us. Think about what encouraging words have done for you.

Encouragement is one of the most powerful human capabilities. Most likely, we have chosen the professions we are in and have some of the skill sets we possess because someone, somewhere, encouraged us in those areas. The root of "encourage" is to bring courage. It means to speak in such a way as to embolden one another to be courageous and not fear.[18] You probably took risks to learn a skill or try something new because someone encouraged you to. We are indeed strengthened toward something when we are encouraged. That's most likely why Paul linked encouragement with a sense of being strengthened in 1 Thessalonians 5:11: "Therefore encourage one another and *build each other up*..." One of the most effective ways we can build the church of Christ is through building people up in love. To do so is to be encouraging.

Years ago, I received a copy of a book called *Balcony People*. The premise of this thin, yet poignant, work is that there are balcony people in our lives and there are basement people in our lives. The people in the "balconies" of our lives "cheer us on, energizing us by their warm affirmations. There are others who live down in the 'basement,' coldly tearing away at our souls with their unfair and critical judgments."[19] As well, we ourselves can either be a person who pulls others to look up, to see things brighter, and to be gutsy, or we can pull others down through disapproving negativity or cold distance. Are you a balcony person in the lives of others, or does an honest look in the mirror show you that people don't necessarily feel your love? Are you doing as God commands and making "*every effort* to do what leads to peace and to mutual edification" (Romans 14:19)? Think now about the initials of the two people you recorded in the first section of this book. Are you a balcony person or a basement person to those people? What would they say about you if asked?

Lest we be misguided in our thinking about what encouragement is, let's be clear. It is not verbal excess or meaningless fluff. Encouragement is not droning on and on endlessly in some honey-tongued rant. Instead, verbal encouragement is like an "apt word" described in Proverbs. Chapter 25 verse 11 says, "A word aptly spoken is like apples of gold in settings of silver." The value of an encouraging apt word is massive. As well, an affirming, comforting, or exhorting word is best when it is pertinent to the situation and well-placed: "A man finds joy in giving an apt reply – and how good is a timely word!" (Proverbs 15:23). Our words are incredibly powerful because we were made in the image of a God who created everything that exists by *speaking* it into being.

Perhaps the proverb that sums it up best is chapter 18, verse 21: "The tongue has the power of life and death, and those who love it will eat its fruit." Like the author of *Balcony People* understood, God has given us the most powerful instrument on earth in the tongue. We can use it to bring life to others or some form of death. And every utterance from our mouths is doing one or the other. There are no innocuous phrases.

While it is true that encouragement is often the spoken word, we have to enlarge our perspective and think about what encourages us personally. Yes, affirming words are a major and important type of encouragement. However, in the broader sense, encouragement can be:

≈ **Remembering the details of someone's life, a situation he told you about, or something he shared with you.** What a blessing it is to a person when you can add a statement like, "Oh, like your Uncle Jack who you told me about last week." I guarantee you will see his eyes light up over the fact that you actually cared enough to remember a detail of his life.

≈ **Following up with someone.** Again, for you to ask, "How did your doctor's appointment go?" or "Did you have a nice visit with your parents?" will touch people deeply because you simply took the time to follow up a previous conversation.

≈ **Being thoughtful.** Bringing a coworker a donut, sending someone a card, or asking if you can take your friend's car to the shop are all thoughtful acts which deeply encourage others.

≈ **Taking an interest.** Moving towards someone with genuine interest in who God has made him or her uniquely to be is abundantly encouraging. "Hey, what's the story behind that tattoo?" and "I heard you went hiking in the Grand Canyon. What was that like?" are two examples of how simply taking an interest in another can be a source of encouragement to his or her soul in a world where self-concern reigns.

Finally, encouragement that is specific is the most effective type of encouragement possible. To tell someone that she is great is uplifting. To tell her she is a wonderful friend also builds up. But to tell her that you were so touched by watching her talk to the stranger in a group over in the corner when no one else had will deeply encourage her – it will lift her up, affirm her sacrifice, embolden her to continue using that gift, and so on. So, while any effort to encourage is wonderful and should be attempted at all times, the most productive type is very specific. Specific encouragement is like using a laser versus a flashlight.

To summarize, the point here is that you can never encourage others too much. So, I have a question for us. Why don't we? Really, why don't you encourage more? Because you fear it won't be reciprocated? Because you fear looking effeminate if you are a male, gushy if you are a female, or just plain loony? Why not be a huge encourager? Fear of doing it wrong? You can't! If our job is to love big – in large ways and like mature people – then why not encourage more? Because you buy into some lie that you don't have much to offer or that someone doesn't care what you think? Really, what do you have to lose by making this adjustment to your life? The Bible records that we are to "encourage one another daily, as long as it is called 'Today,' so that none of you may be hardened by sin's deceitfulness" (Hebrews 3:13). Have you encouraged someone today? Ask yourself why you wouldn't simply go overboard now, even to the point of having a reputation as an outrageous encourager. *You have nothing to lose and everything to gain in taking whatever risks necessary to get outside yourself and encourage others.*

Take whatever risks necessary to encourage others.

Give, not get

To love big is to follow Jesus' words recorded in Luke 9:23-24: "If anyone would come after me, he must deny himself and take up his cross daily and follow me. For whoever wants to save his life will lose it, but whoever loses his life for me will save it." If you are looking for true soul connection in the relationships in your life, you must know clearly that it will not come through trying to get something out of others. Attempting to wrest love from someone else, grappling for attention, or manipulating for affirmation will never work to ascertain true connection with another. Instead, life-giving relationships will only occur as we follow Jesus' teaching to deny ourselves and lose our lives for others. This is the essence of loving large and loving like the big person.

The Luke verses above and myriad others in the Word tell us plainly that we are here on earth to bless others, not to seek to be blessed by them. *We are to look to give rather than get from others.* Talk about loving like the big person! But when we do this, we then often receive the very thing we were looking for in the first place – that's the paradoxical turnabout of sacrifice that Jesus describes – "whoever wants to save his life will lose it, but whoever loses his life…will save it." If you position yourself in every situation to seek to give, you will discover peace, joy, and an indescribable "yes" from the Holy Spirit. While this is so basic on one level, it is so profoundly hard to do in the practical world. We live in a society that rewards self-centeredness. We live in flesh that is constantly being tempted to choose self over another. However, I guarantee that as you methodically begin to change your life to look to give love to others rather than get something from them, you will experience true fellowship with Christ. I think perhaps it's just a tiny portion of what it means to "always carry around in our body the death of Christ" (2 Corinthians 4:10).

What does this mean for you and me practically? Simply put, when you feel you might want some encouraging words, *give them.* When you sense a hug would be nice, *give one.* When you feel a bit like you might be excluded from a group, make some phone calls and initiate an outing to include others. When you wish the phone would ring, pick it up and call a new friend. If you want someone to pray for you, call her and ask how you can pray for her. In other words, the very impulse you have to try to get something out of someone else, turn it around and sacrificially give that very thing to another. Know that God Himself is watching, and He sees you. Giving

Jesus this priority over our own flesh is a beautiful movement, made possible only by His life within us.

The big one

In the previous sections about loving big, the idea of loving like the bigger person has been introduced. To do so is to put on maturity, to seek to interact with others like Christ, and to refuse childish behaviors. The book title *Big Girls Don't Whine* captures this idea.[20] The important realization here is that mature behavior is a choice. To be the big girl or boy

> *Mature behavior is a choice.*

is a decision you must make every time. I can't think of one situation when my response was God-pleasing and others-centered that was not a result of a choice to be mature. Unfortunately, being the little girl or boy comes naturally. Whining, complaining, bickering, gossiping, judging, slacking – these all come much too easily to most of us, don't they? We are virtual pros at picking up our toys and going home. However, because God promises we can "do all things through Christ who strengthens" us (Philippians 4:13), He will certainly honor our efforts to act like the Christian man or woman our actual age reflects.

A challenging reality to comprehend is that some people are actually different emotional ages than their physical ages. So to allow it to sink in, let me say it another way. People can be 30, 40, or 50 years old, but still function emotionally like an eight, ten, or 12 year old. It's true. Why, when you really think about it, do middle-aged business executives collect Match Box cars? Or grown women teddy bears? Have you ever been intimidated by someone in a meeting only to hear him talking afterwards about how he stayed up late drinking with friends, playing Nintendo? While certainly these can be normal hobbies, they can also indicate a younger emotional age. Have you ever found it curious that grown adults who function just fine in society obsess over a comment made by a sales clerk or shut down completely when something doesn't go their way? Just today a client of mine revealed what I have heard countless times as capable, got-it-together people have borne their deepest hearts – "When it all comes down to it, I really just think I want to be held."

This concept can be a bit disturbing or it can bring new understanding. There are times when I have been talking with a 52-year-old man, but carefully paying attention to his emotional capacity at about age eleven. Sometimes I don't share something that's going on in my life with one particular friend, because I know she will always find a way to gossip about someone through it. Another great person I know shouldn't hug women because of where his emotional maturity stopped – adolescence. He can't do it without having his thoughts go completely awry. Generally, people don't know that their emotional age is younger, but given time, anyone who interacts with them on a regular basis can tell. You come to expect Sarah to say, "I just don't get it" when engaged in deeper discussion or Tim to joke around when the conversation moves to serious matters. You realize that Josiah really just wants people to tell him over and over that they like him, and that Trudy always speaks in extremes, that she "hates" this or that.

What does this have to do with true soul connection? First, realizing other people's general emotional age allows you to have appropriate expectations of them. We can have understanding and compassion when we see another's limitations. Second, realizing your own emotional age allows you to see a clearer path of growth for yourself. What age do you feel inside? Perhaps the fact that you feel 18 internally, but are actually 42, is an indicator of being stuck. Relationships can become infinitely more satisfying if you know yourself and have some idea of who the other person really is, not just who you wish he or she was.

People end up being stuck in a younger emotional age for a few different reasons. One is trauma. When a child loses his father in an automobile accident at age 14 and if his mother's ensuing depression, sister's resultant acting out, and grandparent's grief all leave him isolated, he could very well never move beyond that age emotionally. There was no one engaged in helping him grow up. Sexual abuse victims, while exceeding performance expectations in many areas of life, are often hiding the fact that they are very, very emotionally young inside. Another reason people get stuck is that they reach the emotional age of their own parents. Think about the 52-year-old father who is a financial wreck. He never learned to break a cycle of fiscal irresponsibility, so it's not surprising to see his own son stuck in the identical pattern. It's the same with emotional ages. Parents can't generally parent their children's emotional intelligence to a level they have not reached.

Another reason why people get stuck is that they are addicted. The person who chooses numbing out through some substance becomes virtually frozen at the age she began. She isn't engaged in real life anymore because of the escapist urge met through alcohol, pornography, drugs and whatnot. It is commonplace for people struggling with addiction to be quite obviously juvenile. I had a client who routinely asked, "Is that bad? Is that okay?" when beginning to process his emotions, because he quite literally had no concept of mature versus immature thinking.

This discussion highlights the idea of what's called "emotional intelligence." Emotional intelligence "describes an ability, capacity, or skill to perceive, assess, and manage the emotions of one's self, of others, and of groups."[21] Another definition is "the ability to integrate thinking and feeling to make optimal decisions."[22] These definitions tell us that emotion can assist cognition, which is why "people with high emotional intelligence tend to be more successful in life than those with lower [emotional intelligence] even if their classical IQ is average."[23] Being emotionally wise helps us be smarter in all areas of life. For you and me, what's important to take from these thoughts is that people have a different emotional intelligence just like they have a different cognitive intelligence. To learn to perceive another's emotional maturity or immaturity permits us to have appropriate expectations and wise perspectives when dealing with others around us.

Of course, the engaged reader can't help but think, "What emotional age equivalent am I?" This paragraph contains some helpful diagnostic questions. Do you find yourself thinking in extremes: something is this way or that, it's black or white, all or none, always or never? Being a person who thinks in such polarities is not uncommon, but can be an immature way to process the actual world of dynamic people and circumstances. Do you find yourself living for that one, perfect, amazing day in the future when you have defeated your issues and there will be nothing wrong in your life? Such fantasizing for the day when everything will be all right is overwhelmingly encouraged by our society, but can indicate a young emotional level. Are you constantly upset that things don't ever seem to work out for you, or do you find you lack the ability to live outside of what is happening in this particular moment? Is this you: if things in your life are good, then you are good, and if things in your life are bad, then you are depressed? Living in or being caught up in minutia can indicate a lack of ability to have a broader picture on life, which is also sometimes evidence of emotional immaturity. As well, living life from a third person's perspective in which you think everyone is always watching and evaluating you is an early adolescent quality. Is this you? These few examples can help us begin to broaden our understanding of our own and other's emotional intelligence.

One example in my life comes from an amazing person I know. After a period of soul searching, she one day described herself as having what she would consider a "capful" capacity for deep relationships. She pictured a cap from a 2-liter type bottle. Her assessment of my relational capacity is that mine is like a pitcher. Whether the assessment is accurate is not the issue. What I'm trying to highlight is her insight into herself. As she strove to understand herself, it helped her accept her own emotional capability, and subsequently not to compare herself with others. She and I are the closest of friends, and when it comes to various capacities (not just emotional), both of us realize neither one is better than the other. There isn't one more "right" way to be, but as we understand and embrace our differences, our relationship deepens, and trust and respect actually grow. If you can assess another's emotional "age" or capability, then you can often quite literally love like the "big" person. You don't expect your three-year-old not to throw temper tantrums when he doesn't get what he wants, so you can't expect your friend with an emotional intelligence of a 12-year-old to really "be there" for you when you are going through the hardest trial of your life.

Finally, understanding your own level of emotional maturity allows you to seek out others who are more emotionally astute and learn from them. If you can realize you have a tendency to shut down when conflict arises, then you can target how to hang in there and express yourself. If you find that you are an all-or-none thinker, you can work on not being so extreme in your thinking, such as: "Even though x is really bad, a, b, and c are actually good." If you discover you can't accept criticism in any form, you can begin to work on considering the source, agreeing with the feedback, or not generalizing it to mean something it doesn't. Putting an "age" of sorts on your emotional level is helpful, too, because you can look at people that actual age and see what they do that is similar to yourself. My 11-year-old presents an impassioned, vigorous, airtight legal defense for his every move right now. It's the part of the path that he is on emotionally in his journey towards maturity. If he's doing that same thing when he's 27, then we have a problem. Where are you, and what does God want you to glean from this section on loving like the big boy or girl, rather than like the little kid?

One-down is really up

Another life-changing and therefore relationship-changing concept can be found in the idea that "every person is my teacher." This means that your approach to everyone you meet, talk with on a daily basis, and even live with is to regard him as having something valuable to offer. We can learn from every person on the planet, even those we don't respect. In *Don't Sweat the Small Stuff*, Richard Carlson challenges the reader to "imagine that everyone is enlightened except you."[24] Such a perspective promotes humility, and helps us live out Jesus' way, as recorded in Philippians 2:3, 5-7:

"Do nothing out of selfish ambition or vain conceit, *but in humility consider others better than yourselves....* Your attitude should be the same as that of Christ Jesus, who, being in very nature God, did not consider equality with God something to be grasped, but made himself nothing, taking the very nature of a servant..." (italics mine).

"Kenosis" is a Greek word in verse seven ("he made himself nothing"), which means an emptying.[25] To be willing to put yourself in the position to consider others better than you and learn from them is truly a Christ-honoring, love-like-a-big-person act.

The mindset that all other humans have something to teach us is called a one-down approach. This stance towards people is extremely effective. If you want to see your favor with others increase and your communication be more effectual, work hard to have a one-down approach. It is having in your mind that you are following Christ in living out humility. Interacting from a one-down perspective subtly changes your communication to become more palatable to people. You come across as softer, more open, more humble, and actually wiser. To communicate in a one-down perspective means you say phrases like:

- ≈ "This is just my opinion, which is one of many."

- ≈ "I'm not sure, but one answer could be..."

- ≈ "I'll give you my advice, but please feel free to take it or leave it."

- ≈ "I'm certain I don't know every side of this story, but maybe..."

Using words like "could be," "maybe," "I'm not sure," demonstrate your openness to another's way of thinking.

I'm certain that changing your mindset to be one of learning from the other person will bring progress, especially if you are caught in a cycle within a relationship where you can't make any headway. The one-down perspective is modeling the kenosis life of the Lord Jesus for believers. This approach has even been developed in secular arenas to denote a tactic where you put another in the position of power in order to facilitate a certain outcome. It's actually a pretty sophisticated tool in the toolbox of psychology and business, but in the life of Jesus-followers, it is a basic building block for all relationships. It could be said, according to Philippians 2, that the one-down approach is the epitome of what it is to "love big." Dietrich Bonheoffer reminds us why we must live this way: "Our community with one another consists solely on what Christ has done for both of us." We are no better than any other sinner saved by Jesus, and it is beautiful when we live that out.

Assuming the best

Churches are known as the only army that shoots its wounded, which is sad, but all too often true. I have been more deeply hurt in my life by Christians than by non-Christians and I know countless others who have had the same experience. Quite seriously, I had someone call me this very morning and beg me to write a book to help believers in their relationships. She recounted situation after situation in churches where people started out close and unified until invariably something happened that led to a permanent drift or split. It is truly grievous that division can topple those of us in Christ. We have the Spirit of Christ within us! It makes me want to rise up and rally believers everywhere to stop this trend and reverse this reality. Certainly, the attack on Christian relationships is intense because such God-glorifying potentialities are focal points for the powers of hell. However, let this fact fuel and empower us to truly be the overcoming people that Christ's death makes possible for us! Let's love so big as to leave an imprint on everyone with whom we come in contact.

With that little sermonette in mind, let's continue looking at how we can truly love big. Simply put, to reverse any relationally distressing trend, *we need to choose to believe the best*. Our problem is that we too often assume anything but the best about each other – second-guessing, mistrusting, doubting motives, and personalizing innocent comments. Instead, we need to follow God's admonition to us in Romans 12:10: "Be devoted to one another in brotherly love. Honor one another above yourselves." Being devoted to one another in love, or loving big, is abetted by our willingness to make grace-based assumptions about each other in the absence of full knowledge.

Why should we assume the best? Charles Swindoll, in his classic work *Grace Awakening*, elucidates how extending grace to others has a huge impact.[26] He explains that we don't ever know the whole story about anybody or anything. We don't know what it's like to be someone else, with that past, that personality, those looks, that spouse, that job, those hurts, and that family of origin. We *never* know fully what another is thinking and feeling and why. The cranky person in the grocery line could have just been given news of a terminal illness. The person who looks like she's not engaged in the conversation might be deaf in one ear. The friend who can't watch horror movies might have been robbed at gunpoint as a child. Do you know that many men who become extreme body builders were sexually violated as children? No one's situation is ever fully as it seems outwardly.

Though he has preached to thousands, Swindoll recounts being a bit irritated at a couple who sat in the front row at every session of a conference. The male would instantly fall asleep and snooze throughout the message. At the end of the event, the couple approached Chuck and thanked him deeply for his messages, explaining that they had just found out the man had cancer and would likely die in short order. Their choice whether to come or not had been a difficult one, and they were thankful they had come. We never know why a person is doing what he is doing, even if we think we can assess it accurately.

Choosing to assume the best is extending God's grace horizontally. We do so because we can't read another person's motives. To fully perceive someone's motives while looking at him or her from the outside in is unattainable. It's also impossible to be entirely objective. Finally, we assume the best rather than the worst because we ourselves are imperfect and inconsistent. However, we so often forget our own shortcomings and in the absence of clarity assume the worst about our friend. We do these things because we unconsciously put our standards on other people and assume our situations are fairly similar. Do you think of the friend who passes you by without recognition in the church foyer, "What is wrong with her? What did I ever do to her? I can't believe she'd ignore me like that!" or "Wow, something must be wrong because it's so unlike her to not see me. Maybe it was a bad morning with the kids, she's not feeling well, or she just found out some bad news." The second response might even lead us to do what is God's plan for our friendships – to pray for that friend! However, we won't be anywhere near that kind of graceful support if we don't first assume the best rather than the worst.

Another practical outworking of this concept of assuming the best is this: don't overpersonalize. Believe it or not, it's not about you. We have such a tendency to interpret an unreturned phone call, choppy text, or to-the-point email as somehow about us. We will lay awake at night wondering why someone said what she did. We will obsess about how others perceive us and become offended or insulted at the smallest miscue. Those are ways we live like emotional children. Occasionally, it is true that the situation is about us, but until we know for certain, learning to not personalize situations is one of the best ways we can love like the big, or mature, person. When the pastor asks another person to chair the search committee even though you tossed your hat in the ring to do so, don't take it personally. When two families that are both friends of yours get together for dinner and your family isn't invited, assume the best, not the worst. If a Christian co-worker seems to cool off on communication with you, don't overpersonalize. It is often something completely unrelated to you that is going on with the other person. Choose that perspective until you find out differently. Assume the best scenario, not the worst.

However, when you just can't shake it, or perhaps you even have discernment from the Holy Spirit, and it seems like there is something amiss that does concern you, then it is time to question. One of the most helpful relationship protectors is *"when in doubt, check it out."* If assuming the best still doesn't quell a nipping concern or nagging thought, then ask. When you really don't know why someone made a certain choice in regards to something concerning you, then check it out. For example: "Hey, I could be really off-base here, but I noticed we haven't been talking as much lately. Is something up?" or "Can I check something out with you? I wasn't sure if you were upset with me yesterday or if something else was going on." (Did you notice the one-down posture in these questions?)

The admonition "when in doubt, check it out" is a great tool to have in your relationship toolbox. It can actually have a huge impact in marriages, too. So often where those daily life-on-life relationships go wrong (like with marriages and families) is when we begin making negative assumptions based on past hurts and behaviors. Try working very hard to assume the best, and then commit to checking it out when you are truly in doubt and see what begins to happen in those close relationships. These are excellent tactics to maintain true soul connection.

Another such approach is to "walk it off" when something happens that could send a relationship in a bad direction. I love this phrase because it's visually compelling to think about. When I was together with a group of friends recently, in the jumble of group interaction, I heard one of my friends say some remark about me that caught my attention. He did it with a smile on his face. He is a very true friend of mine, and what he said was actually probably true. So, instead of allowing it to hurt my feelings, I decided instead to "walk it off" much the same way football players do with a stinger in a football game. They walk around a bit, shake out the place of hurt, and move on to the next play. Emotionally, we can do this as well. When someone says something that you could become offended or hurt by, stop and evaluate, "Is this really something worth making into a bigger deal? In the scheme of life, does this really do that much damage?" When the answer is "no," just assume the best, shake it off, and move on. So very many things in life are simply not worth the internal energy we give them. Training ourselves to "walk it off" is another way we can love big because we know we have been loved completely and totally by One who never fails.

Safe zone

When I was in elementary school, the neighborhood "safe house" movement began. Neighbors agreed that if a child was lost or in danger, he or she could go to the houses with identifiable markers in their windows and an adult would be there to help. I remember learning that if I couldn't find my way or was in trouble, I could go to the houses with the yellow signs and they would help me. When I think of true soul connections, I am reminded of those safe signs. Feeling safe is a critical component of the best relationships. My doctoral research was on authentic encounters, and I have been counseling others for many years. At every turn, whether my own studies or others, whether in the church or social settings, whether with individuals or groups, it does not matter – it is a fact that safety is an inherent part of what people consider to be rewarding relationships.

The idea of safety is that of being someone on whom others can depend for certain things. A safe person is one who is respectful of your feelings, thoughts, and values. A safe person is one who listens well. A safe person is one who refrains from quick judgment and instead seeks to understand. A safe person is a person of his or her word. Someone safe knows how to "rejoice with those who rejoice; mourn with those who mourn" (Romans 12:15). A safe friend is just that – safe. He or she is cautious when handling valuables – another's thoughts, feelings, opinions, dreams, hurts, fears, aspirations. He or she is consistent, not a person who is so volatile that you don't know what to expect from one day to the next. Someone who is safe for you is the type of person you call when times get tough, someone you know will pray for you, speak God's truth, and remind you of important realities, all in love. He or she doesn't feel compelled to give pat answers or hollow words. Comfortable silence is the hallmark of a relationship that is safe.

When I picture how a safe person handles another's words, I see a pair of hands cupped, like holding something valuable or water from a faucet. The safe friend treasures every word, every minute spent together, and every emotion shared like one would hold a blown glass figurine. Sometimes when I'm listening to someone, I visualize this, especially when this person communicates in a fashion different than mine. We do this because we sincerely believe people bear the image of God, are one-of-a-kind unique, and are given us by God to love and enjoy. We understand that each human person is a treasure, created by God for good works (2 Corinthians 4:7, Ephesians 2:10). A safe person is not wimpy, unwilling to say hard things, or untruthful. He or she is strong enough to be discerning, wise enough to know when to speak and when not to, and courageous enough to comfort someone. Safe people are the strongest people around.

Something surprising and important to note is that there is a poison in relationships almost all of us have injected at some point or another. People don't know it's poison, but when it enters into communication, it begins to deteriorate the safety of relationships. Another problem with this poison is that many of us find it enjoyable to use. We don't see how damaging it is. This poison is why stand-up comedians and class clowns are often some of the most popular, yet lonely, people on the face of the planet. This devastating toxin to true soul connection? Sarcasm and mockery.

Our immediate reaction to this might be "Come on! Sarcasm is hilarious. Some of the funniest people I know use sarcasm in their humor." This is true. I myself enjoy some types of sarcasm immensely. However, mockery and sarcasm fritter away at relational safety. When you become known as a sarcastic person, you will also be perceived as a person that is unsafe. Think about it. Is there someone you know who is sarcastic with whom you feel comfortable sharing your fears and struggles? Probably not. There's just something about the unpredictable nature of sarcastic people that repels people looking for true relationships. Perhaps it's found somehow in the truth of this proverb: "A soothing tongue is a tree of life, but perversion in it crushes the spirit" (Proverbs 15:4 NASB). While sarcasm is not necessarily perverse, it is a perversion, never mind the fact that it is not soothing. So, take from it what you will, but know that an unanticipated and unintentional side effect of your sarcastic humor is that people will be less likely to consider you safe.

Huge love

This chapter on loving big has presented many components. "Big" is a type of measurement. To measure love is impossible, but is seen in examples like this: Do you have a tender concern for the welfare of one who treats you wrongly? The person who loves big is never blind to other's faults. He or she sees people clearly, but does not judge. He or she forgives, accepts and assumes God is working in other's lives and continues to be warmly involved.[27] Amy Carmichael offers a piercing picture of what it is to love big: "If I can enjoy a joke at the expense of another, if I can in any way slight another in conversation or even in thought, then I know nothing of Calvary love."[28] To love like Jesus at Calvary is to show grace in the face of another's sin.

To love big is in many ways to choose to walk in the "look beyond" stance we described in chapter one. It is to encourage in voluminous amounts. At a bare minimum, it is to encourage more today than you have ever before. It is to look to give and not get, and to quite literally choose to be the bigger person (and not in a bitter or haughty way). Loving big involves assuming the best and not overpersonalizing, but "walking it off."

When we can't, we check it out when in doubt. One with the heart to love big seeks to be a safe person, one who is accepting and forgiving rather than closed and grudge bearing. To love big is to quite literally love as big as you possibly can – demonstratively, prayerfully, with words, with actions, with all of the you that you can muster. When you enter a room, are people excited because they know you will seek to love big, or are they tentative, because they don't really know what you think of them? To love big is to be intense and intentional in communicating the love of God to every person you meet. It's also to love like the biggest (most mature) person in a situation. In these ways, we bless others with a healing dose of the love of Christ.

A Henri Nouwen thought gives the perfect summary of the posture presented in this chapter:

> "When we honestly ask ourselves which person in our lives means the most to us, we often find that it is those who, instead of giving advice, solutions, or cures, have chosen rather to share our pain and touch

our wounds with a warm and tender hand. The friend who can be silent with us in a moment of despair or confusion, who can stay with us in an hour of grief and bereavement, who can tolerate not knowing, not curing, not healing and face with us the reality of our powerlessness, that is a friend who cares."

Chapter Three
LISTEN LOTS

The Bible gives one of its most succinct relational directives by saying, "Everyone should be quick to listen, slow to speak, and slow to become angry" (James 1:19). Learning to truly listen in our noise-filled, information-overloaded, activity-laden society is a lost art. Becoming an excellent listener, however, cannot only change the lives of those around you, it can also change your life. God gave us two ears and only one mouth for a pragmatic reason. We should listen twice as much as we speak.

A few years back, I was asked to speak to a group of people who had dedicated themselves to helping youth. I greatly admired these sacrificial saints, and the task of investing in their lives was daunting. I wanted to be confident that I wasn't wasting their valuable time. To prepare, I spent a few weeks surveying every student with whom I came in contact, including ones on the street. I asked them what they most wanted out of the adults in their lives or what impacted them the most about their favorite people. Overwhelmingly, these teens responded that they wanted and appreciated someone who really listens. The pervasiveness of the answer was shocking. Over and over I heard that adolescents feel most valued and understood when they are really listened to. What was unsaid but equally as obvious was that these people also gained permission to speak into the students' lives by their willingness to truly *hear*.

Listening versus hearing

There is indeed a difference between listening to someone and actually hearing him or her. Frankly, most people in conversation are simply waiting to speak. We all know ones who can't even wait, but interrupt and dominate in conversations. However, those of us who are more polite on the outside can be just the same as that person on the inside. We often listen until we have something to react to, something to share knowledge about, or some similar story. When we have listened long enough to hear our entry point, we then simply hold on for as long as it takes that person to finish his or her thought. That is not actually hearing. It is more like self-centered listening. Just waiting to speak or share your own opinion does not mean that you are apprehending what another is trying to communicate.

Because listening does not come naturally to most of us, it is a skill that has to be developed. Most people talk at the rate of 120 words per minute, whereas most spoken language can be comprehended well at rates up to 250 words per minute.[29] This discrepancy allows plenty of extra time for mental activity. What we do with that mental space is the difference between listening and hearing. Usually a person hears only about 20% of what is said. The rest of the time we can kill time waiting to speak, which exposes the underlying belief that what you have to say is the most important part of the conversation. We often listen piecemeal just until we have something to react to or hang in there just long enough to hear an idea which brings up a topic on which we can discourse.

We can even be waiting to argue, or even worse, listening to judge. We're not actually replying to what another has said, but often even interpret his or her motives and wait simply to supply our judgments freely. Instead, we need to listen before we evaluate. Solomon recorded this truth in a society not nearly as frenetic as our own: "He who answers before listening – that is his folly and his shame" (Proverbs 18:13). Do you answer before really listening?

One of the fundamental elements of effective listening is simply waiting patiently while others talk. While this may seem simple to us, the reality is that Christ-focused relationships involve a continual willingness to sacrifice for others. Truly listening involves the same choice. It is tough to listen, especially to a known talker. It is hard to make yourself really focus on someone when you have 15 other places to be. However, these basic principles and truths, if executed, can bring a level of meaning and peace to your life and relationships that is otherwise not experienced. Paul Tournier said, "How beautiful, how grand and liberating this experience is when people learn to help each other. It is impossible to overemphasize the immense need humans have to be really listened to."[30] It's true. The choice to become an excellent, and I'll use the word "godly," listener is, at its core, a sacrificial one. You choose another above yourself. To do so is to follow the example of Christ. Giving another person your time and undivided attention is one of the most powerful ways in today's world to demonstrate genuine love and concern.

Authors Crabb and Allender encourage us to "listen so profoundly that people who tell you their stories begin to believe that whatever matters to them matters to you. Help them to believe it because it's true."[31] This fantastic quote causes us to face the question, "*Do I* really care?" Listening, as we see in the example of Jesus time and again, is truly a sacrificial act. Actually perceiving another person's meaning in communication means that our attention is focused on him, we are excited about what he is going to share, and we feel privileged that he would share with us. Most of us don't really listen because we aren't honestly *primarily* concerned about another. Our chief concern is *me*: "Do I like what she's saying?" "Is he noticing how nice I'm being for listening so well?" "Aren't they going to think I am so smart when I share my opposing viewpoint or latest tidbit on the subject?" The apostle Paul records poignantly that we have a choice in our relationships – to consider ourselves above another or vice versa. "Your attitude should be the same as that of Christ Jesus, who, being in very nature God, did not consider equality with God something to be grasped, but made himself nothing, taking the very nature of a servant" (Philippians 2:5-7). Listening is a way in which we can consider others as better than ourselves.

Active, not passive

While it is a fact that listening is a critical part of any good relationship, it is also a fact that being an excellent listener takes practice. However, because believers house the Spirit of God, they can become extremely effective listeners with just a little work. In other words, it's not out of reach for you to quickly become known as a wonderful person to talk to because of how well you listen! The main component of being a good listener actually has to do with keeping the conversation going. True hearing involves an active, not passive, stance.

One of the main tools for effective listening is to summarize, or paraphrase. Practically, this is to reflect back what another person seems to be communicating. Summarizing involves putting the other person's main points into your own words and sending those thoughts back in a constructive way. Picture holding a mirror up to someone so he can see what he is sharing. From this example, you can see how this skill is also referred to as "reflecting." Reflecting can deal with both the content of what the other person has said as well as the associated feelings. "Content" is the actual data of what a person shared. "Feelings" refers to any emotions accompanying the data. To attempt to reflect back, or summarize, the content or feeling of what another person has said is very effective for communicating love and interest. Here are some examples of statements that summarize content:

≈ This situation has created a lot of problems for you and your family.

≈ You must really care about this project.

≈ So, your office situation is requiring a lot more time than they told you it would.

In situations of conflict, reflecting content is a tremendously valuable tool for working towards resolution, although it requires swallowing one's pride and is laborious to do. Some phrases that are specifically helpful for working through differences of opinion are:

≈ The way you see it then is...

≈ You heard me say...

≈ You think that the situation began by...

≈ You were upset by...

≈ The situation is hurtful or bothersome to you because...

Summarizing another's content and reflecting it back to him is a valuable others-focused listening tool.

Reflecting back feelings is essentially doing the same as paraphrasing content, but instead focuses on feeding back to someone what you perceive his or her feelings to be. This could be either because he or she stated those feelings or you can sense them. Whatever the case, focusing on the feelings is important because they are often just as important as the actual content of what a person is saying. Sometimes, they're actually more important. When someone is distraught, for instance, *what* he is saying is often illogical, but the emotion he's suggesting is very legitimate. This is troublesome to people who are heavily rational or cognitive-oriented, but it is a reality that feelings can make or break relationships. This is especially crucial if the distraught person is receiving the message that his emotions are not considered valid. Many marriages struggle from this differential. Instead of attending to how one partner felt in an interaction, fights will often revolve around the particulars of a certain situation, to no avail. Have you ever noticed that no amount of "this happened, then I said this, then you said this" resolves anything? Reflecting back feelings at such a time is a wiser choice. I think most people will be shocked at the relational mileage this gains them. Here are some examples of a person's statement, and what it sounds like to reflect back feelings:

> **Statement**: I read my devotional all the time, but it doesn't make any difference.

> **Response**: Sounds as if you're feeling discouraged.

Statement: I don't really think any of the small groups are for me – they all seem full anyhow.
Response: Seems as though you are feeling like you don't belong or like there's not a place for you.

Statement: I just made the assumption that you would call back this afternoon like you told me.
Response: I get the impression I've really disappointed you.

Some general examples of feeling-focused reflections would be:

- ≈ It sounds as if you're feeling…

- ≈ I get a picture of…

- ≈ Could it be that…?

- ≈ You must feel…

- ≈ It seems as if…

- ≈ That must have been…

- ≈ What I hear you saying is…

- ≈ I get the sense that…

- ≈ I gather…

Lest you have already decided you can't do this because of the overly emotional people with whom you interact, you need to remember that reflecting feelings does not require that you agree with what the other person says. It simply reveals whether or not you comprehend another person's thoughts and feelings and thereby opens the way for further dialogue. Again, your opinion is not of utmost import in conversation.

Another person's perceptions are real, even if they are not based on fact. Therefore, if someone says, "You don't even care about how this has affected me," it usually does little good to respond, "That's not true." Instead, even if you believe another person's perceptions are wrong, take him or her seriously and use clarifying and reflecting responses to gain more insight and to show that you are getting the message. This will continue dialogue to a point where true understanding will occur. At that point, souls are being connected and practically anything can be shared when someone senses genuine non-judgmental attention.

If you have the right motive here, you can't go wrong. Even if you reflect back what you think is a feeling someone is having and it isn't the right one, the relational points you've gained by trying will offset the fact that it was the wrong guess. When you say, "That must have made you mad," and your friend responds, "No, I was actually just frustrated," you have still met your goal to keep conversation going and communicate genuine interest. There's no perfection here! Trying something to improve in this area is always better than doing nothing! Most effective listeners are people who take a stab at addressing the potential things that aren't being said or the deeper issue at hand. For instance, if a person is complaining about her mother-in-law, you can actually help steer her in a less sinful direction while still reflecting back possible feelings. You could say, "It sounds like that's a tough space for you to feel accepted in," or "I'm sure you struggle with how to love her with the love of Christ." Are you getting the gist that I don't want you to be bogged down in the "how," I simply want you to TRY! In doing so, God will get much glory in addition to equipping you for the moment.

Continuing the conversation

So far, we have discussed the power of summarizing (or paraphrasing) and reflecting the content and feelings of another person's words. Another handy tool in the "hearing, not just listening" toolbox is that of clarifying questions. Again, clarifying questions communicate a level of interest and engagement that stir another person deeply. Most people walk around life feeling unimportant, alone, and like people don't really care. So, to encounter a person who tracks well enough in conversation to ask clarifying questions is energizing – even healing. And you and I can be that in the life of another simply by caring enough to listen well and ask a few questions!! Clarifying questions pick up on some portion of what another is sharing and ask for more detail or information about it. Examples of clarifying questions include:

≈ Are you saying…?

≈ Tell me more about…

≈ Can you give me an example?

≈ I'm confused about…

≈ How do you feel about that?

≈ Let me see if I understand…

≈ He said what to you?

≈ What were you thinking when that happened?

≈ How on earth did you handle that?

≈ We are talking about your aunt from Florida, right?

≈ Your boss has been with the company for how long?

≈ So, your sister's children spend a whole week with you in the summer?

Words like these show that you are hearing and thinking about what is being said. Because they also show your interest in getting further information, they encourage the other person to share emotions and perceptions more fully.

To synopsize, questions help us *hear*. Not only do they show we are engaged, caring, and willing to choose another person above ourselves, they allow us to send others life-changing messages like "you matter," "your thoughts are valuable," "your feelings are important." The point is to listen well enough that the conversation continues long enough to allow another person to feel truly heard. As I've said, what I do not want is for you to think this is too complex or hard. What is being suggested here are merely tips for how to live out a sacrificial stance in active conversation. So, even if you can't remember any of the tools being offered here, *everyone* can:

≈ Maintain eye contact

≈ Raise your eyebrows at an interesting part of the conversation

≈ Say "And?" to encourage a person to keep talking

≈ Offer a "Wow!" at the end of a story (or "That must have been something!" or "Crazy!")

≈ Say "Really?!" in agreement with someone's shock or concern

Those are bare minimum things you can do right now with the next person with whom you speak. Eye contact alone will increase your effectiveness in your connections with others. It's disturbing, really, how little even married people really look each other in the eye. I am so excited to think about how effective you are going to not only be, but also feel, in your interactions with others in the upcoming days!

As a side note, there are actually a few types of questions that can shut down a conversation. The two types of conversations to steer away from are yes/no questions and "why?" questions. Yes/no questions provide less information than open-ended ones, and simply provide a stop in dialogue. That is counterproductive to our overarching goal of listening to hear beyond words to true understanding. "Why" questions also tend to shut people down. I'm not quite sure why, other than that they go to people's motives, which is threatening. Consider "Why did you do that?" While it really could be a very harmless and innocent question, there's something about it that causes immediate defensiveness in us. So, while there's nothing inherently wrong with yes/no or "why" questions, they do tend to inhibit, rather than release, sharing.

More than words can tell

You'll likely be stunned at how much truly listening can change things. If you have a child with whom you feel like you're battling, try some of the tools in this chapter. If you are discouraged that you and your spouse just don't seem connected, think about whether you are putting his or her interests above your own in your interactions. Most people just want to be listened to. Don't you? Many wives become frustrated with their "fix-it" husbands who don't seem to really hear what they are saying, but instead begin offering advice or solutions. If you simply want to be listened to (which is a valid desire), then you need to communicate this at the outset of the conversation, rather than after the dialogue has begun to go south.

A bottom line thought in listening can be captured through the question "What is this person really trying to tell me?" To listen for intention is the best compass for how to truly hear. What a person intends to say is often very different than the words he or she uses. Have you ever noticed how human language really falls miserably short in capturing the truest and deepest experiences in life? I get frustrated with human language, especially when attempting to express how the Lord is working in my life, or an incredibly meaningful insight from Him. Perhaps because it's just that – *human* language!! I've come to understand that the deepest things of the Lord are truly *in*expressible. Human words can't begin to depict God's beauty, His ways, His thoughts, His movement. I believe this is why Paul talks about having a joy inexpressible in 1 Peter 1:8. God's joy is not a human capability. It's a spiritual, holy transaction given by an almighty God.

While this might seem like a tangent, my point is simply to underscore that truly listening helps us hear what is or is not being said. There are multiple reasons we need to attempt to listen beyond the words. For instance, one word can mean drastically different things to two different people. Knowing that words and phrases used by people can't accurately capture what they might be trying to communicate helps reinforce our need to listen for someone's intention. Just as the focus of chapter one was to encourage looking beyond any external presentation to one's heart, others-centered listening portrays the same sentiment. With the tools in this chapter, you can get beyond the surface issues, and discern more clearly underlying concerns, motives, and feelings.

You can't do it, though, if you're not listening beyond mere words.

Do you really want to know?

Finally, you might ask how we are to concentrate on listening when someone comes to us to ask us our opinion. Here's a little hint. If someone asks you a question once, he or she usually isn't looking for advice, but for affirmation. It's true. Unfortunately, most people in our culture today are too self-oriented to actually consider they might need instruction. However, people will often ask what someone else's opinion is or what that particular person would do. Again, I say, usually he or she doesn't really want your expertise. They just want your approval. To consider this, play out the following scenario in your head. Someone asks you for advice and you give it, but he clearly isn't interested in what you are sharing or have to offer. The conversation ends with both of you feeling a little "icky" about it. "How did that go wrong?" you wonder. "Did I say something he disagrees with?" Try giving out affirmation next time and see how things change.

Here's the clue to know when someone really wants your advice: If, after receiving your affirmation, someone asks you for your advice again, then he or she really wants the answer. In general for any question, when a people ask twice, they really want your opinion or to know what you think. I do this all the time. I especially don't answer the void-of-any-real-meaning question, "How are you?" on the first go-round. When offered that greeting, I'll say something like, "What is going on in your world?" or "It's my awesome friend!" or "Would you look who God has me crossing paths with." Extremely few people will follow up and ask again, "How are you?" The ones that do, though, I know really want to know. While I don't advocate that kind of avoidant behavior in general, the larger point I'm trying to make is that questions can be like bait. If we take the bait too early, we can unintentionally shut down a conversation.

If we go too quickly to answering surface questions, then we lose the larger opportunity for deeper connection and more profound understanding of another. To reach our goal of having soul relationships, we must seize opportunities to keep conversations open and moving. The question/answer pattern of discussion is effective for the gathering of knowledge, but not effective for the processing of life at any meaningful level. Let's take the example of the seemingly obvious question that someone wants you to answer: "What do you think I should do?" Next time someone asks you, follow it up with "What are you leaning towards?" That person will then speak a bit about his thought processes. You have kept the conversation open and moving rather than shut it down with your answer. Can you see the difference in the dialogues below?

> **Question:** What do you think I should do?
>
> **Response:** I think you really ought to take that job. It'll bring in more money, your wife will be happy with you, and there's more opportunity for advancement.

> **or**
>
> **Question:** What do you think I should do?
>
> **Response:** Well, what kind of thoughts have you been having about it all?

Which one of those demonstrates the attitude of considering others' interests (and opinions!) above our own?

Continuing on with this example, you could answer the "What should I do?" question with a statement of affirmation like, "Well, I see a few options. I'm confident you, God, and the Holy Spirit will figure it out." If a person was not really looking for your advice, the conversation will move away from your opinion. However, if after the person has processed your open probe and asks you again, "But what do you think I should do?", then she really wants to know.

Withholding your personal opinion until you are certain someone is asking for it is a very wise move. First, it keeps you in a humble posture. Second, it provides an avenue to die to yourself, which is always productive. Third, it prevents you from getting a reputation of being opinionated or pressing your own agenda. Such a posture has shown someone that your real agenda is an others-centered understanding. Have you ever noticed that people care most about the quietest person's opinion rather than the one who talks a lot? It's the same principle. A person gains credibility by the willingness to withhold offering his or her opinion until asked. Being a patient listener and wise question-asker engenders respect – maybe because we all know how hard it is to have such self-control!

To this point, Proverbs 1:5 urges, "Let the wise listen and add to their learning and let the discerning get guidance." If you are wise, you will apply yourself to listening, which begets all sorts of learning, understanding, and discernment. The thrust of this book thus far is clearly looking to become less self-oriented for the sake of more godly relationships. In doing so, those relationships will be more fulfilling than they presently are. Though you may doubt that something as seemingly simple or elementary as listening can radically alter your closest relationships, think again.

Chapter Four
LET GO OF FEAR

Any book written about walking in the way of Christ must contain the admonition that Jesus spoke more than any other: *"Do not fear."* How much more do we need this as we talk about relationships! There are more instances in the Word where we are told not to be afraid than any other instruction. Being told not to fear is a necessary focal point for us overanxious, over-controlling, overwrought humans. It really couldn't be any truer, either, that one of the biggest hurdles to having soul connections with others is the presence of fear. So much of what goes on in our relationships is really because of fear. Whatever form it takes, fear gets in the way of the relationships we really want. We must learn to recognize when fear is stifling our relationships, then zero in to conquer it.

Perhaps you find yourself objecting to the assumption that we all have fear as we approach relationships. If so, maybe the idea that each person does whatever he or she can to avoid pain will connect better with you. We are a culture seriously intent on escaping pain. These two realities always live in tension – that we yearn to relate deeply with others, but we are equally compelled to avoid pain at all costs. Good relationships by design involve pain. Look at the beauty of childbirth – ouch! Life on this earth is difficult.

Therefore, as we relate with other humans (made in the image of God, yet still in the flesh), we will have our feelings hurt, be betrayed, feel let down, etc. To expect relationships to be void of these things is both unrealistic and immature. It's akin to fantasizing! The real world of good, fulfilling relationships involves a willingness to stay in there whenever something troublesome occurs, continuing to move toward the other person in love and understanding. Then, on the other side of the issue, the trust level has grown and the bond is tighter. *This* is why standing up and facing our fear of being hurt is worth it as far as relationships go.

Drop the defense

We won't get anywhere in any relationship if we don't want to be hurt. Said another way, if you have a strong commitment to self-protection, you will never have satisfying relationships. Self-protection is doing whatever we can to keep ourselves from being hurt or disappointed by others. It is playing it safe, not letting others know you well, and refusing to ever be vulnerable. We self-protect through changing the subject, remaining aloof, cracking a joke, being super busy, being super spiritual, being indirect. There are innumerable ways we can try to hide from others. We also keep from being open by sharing only small amounts of ourselves even with significant friends, being unavailable to participate in social events, and consistently talking about the superficial. Asking ourselves, "How do I erect fences in my relationships with others?" is a great move toward recognizing self-protection.

> *Self-protection sabotages satisfying relationships.*

There are myriad reasons we self-protect. Some of us have been so wounded in life that we have learned being vulnerable in any way will result in serious abuse. Others have been left by the parent who swore he'd never divorce. Still others have just borne the brunt of an all-out hellish assault to their trust in others, leaving it practically irreparable. Getting believers to self-protect is a primary aim of evil. Why? Because, as we observed in the introduction, God is glorified in loving, authentic relationships. Self-protection kills authenticity.

This is likely why Larry Crabb's work on this topic struck such a chord. In his seminal work *Inside Out*, he referred to self-protection as sin.[32] Not just the result of hurt in a person's life. Not just a common temptation with which people struggle. Not just something that keeps us from being overwhelmed in our emotional existence. A *sin*. At its root is self-preservation. It is a refusal to believe that God will protect us. Instead, in essence, it is telling God, "While I trust You with other areas, I've got this one. I'm not so crazy about how you handled these types of situations for me in the past, so I need to take care of myself here." Really, is your trust in God or is your trust in yourself when it comes to how you face relationships?

Crabb describes how self-protection is the "silent killer of community." This is because it violates the law of love. "If the core business of life is to love each other as God loves us, then a priority effort to play it safe interferes with the purpose of living."[33] While not intentional, we so fear getting hurt that we often try to manipulate others to get them to act or speak in ways so we won't be rejected. We are not to walk around guarded in our own little fortresses. (And then wonder why we're so lonely all the time!) Instead, our trust is in Christ – He is our significance; He is our meaning. It means believing that the Father will not allow anything to happen to us that He will not use to strengthen, heal, and comfort us. Jesus extended his heart and was trusting even to those He *knew* would betray Him. Think about that. If you knew one of your closest friends was going to completely devastate you this week, can you imagine continuing to extend yourself in love and entrusting him with your thoughts until then? Clearly, our self-protective patterns interfere with our willingness to move towards others with *their* well-being in view.

True soul connection requires a shift in motivation from self-preservation to an abandoned trust that my life is not my own, and God can do whatever He wants with me. We cannot have the kinds of relationships we are designed for and long for if we are living in fear and self-protection. Letting go of self-protection is a huge step towards letting go of fear. This does not mean we stupidly expose ourselves to avowedly evil or vengeful people. It just means that those whose trust is in God do not fear what others can do to them. We live out the truth, "In God I trust; I will not be afraid. What can man do to me?" (Psalm 56:11)

Fear it or face it

If letting go of fear is crucial to having quality connections with others, then there is one such fear we must confront head-on. For whatever reason, it seems that fear of conflict has become a garden-variety issue for many people. While there are certainly those edgy individuals who seek out conflict, for the majority of us, the idea of having disagreements is uncomfortable. For some people, it is paralyzing. They will completely orchestrate their lives to avoid it at all costs. And again, while I'm definitely not saying we need to be excited about relational clashes, we need to stop bowing to the god of conflict!! To function in such a weak way is to minimize the Spirit of God who is pulsating strength through us at all times. We have been given the ministry of reconciliation (2 Corinthians 5:18). Therefore, we are not walking in God's ways if we aren't willing to be around anything or anyone in need of reconciliation – with Him or with others.

I'll never forget the chapter heading of a book I once read. The title alone was instructive. It was, "Conflict: A Pathway to Intimacy."[34] It's a true statement. When we have a conflict with another, especially a spouse or family member, and if we will hang in there and *work the whole way through it,* we'll probably be surprised at what happens. Intimacy can be defined as "into-me-you-see," and when we work through differences, much of our insides are seen! Talking, seeking to understand, believing the best, checking out assumptions – all of these will reap positive consequences when we do them. If we refuse to withdraw or run at the first sign of conflict, we are setting ourselves up to have a deeper relationship in the future. Why? Because we ultimately come to trust that other person more than before. Quite an amazing finish to what starts out threatening to be a relationship wrecker. It's probably why wise Solomon said, "The end of a matter is better than its beginning and patience is better than pride" (Ecclesiastes 7:8).

Don't get me wrong – I know it is tough business to force yourself to do this. Even as I write, I am in the middle of a relational strain. (Try living this stuff as you write a book about it!!) However, I trust that continuing to press in and talk and love and ask questions will bring us closer because I've lived it before. I've seen God's faithfulness to His idea – loving our neighbors as ourselves. When we press into loving relationships, He will bless. When we continue on despite trepidation and uncertainty, He will speak and strengthen. Why? Because "there is no fear in love. But perfect love drives out fear, because fear has to do with punishment. The one who fears is not made perfect in love" (1 John 4:18). Moving toward a tough relationship in sacrificial love will drive out fear.

Continuing to love when the going gets rough in a relationship is living out the admonition to "not love with words or tongue, but with actions and in truth" (1 John 3:18). My closest friends are those with whom I have been through tough times, including relational struggles. So the next time your husband or wife or mother or friend or coworker gets upset with you, boldly love with a forgiving and understanding heart and watch the intimacy level of your relationship increase.

Stand in

So much of true soul connecting happens if we can develop thicker skin. Unfortunately, most of us are just pretty immature in our relationships. Are we really rooted in Christ Jesus? Do we really believe all that God says? If so, we'll be stronger and less immature as we interact closely with others. So much about the principles for living recorded in the New Testament epistles instructs us to be stronger and less dependent upon people for our significance. Instead, we are to look at people through generous, giving, and gracious eyes, not through the lens of how they can benefit us. Many times the Word exhorts us to "stand firm," "be strong and courageous," and sometimes simply to "stand."[35] Can you "stand" in relationship? Will you?

Mike developed a three-punch rule a few years into our relationship, although I shudder to think about how a reader might perceive that statement. It's not what it sounds like! Since he is more cognitive and categorical in his processing and I am more emotional and layered, our communication has been tricky. At times, when trying to express my feelings, I would speak in a way that sounded extreme or worse, critical, to Mike. This would quickly discourage him, since he sometimes receives things to a greater degree than I intend. As a result, he would "check out" of the conversation, and then I would be discouraged that we were never going to make progress in our communication.

At some point he realized that if he could just "stand in" whenever he felt like the first hard statement came, our relationship would be helped. Then, as he would stand and stay in the conversation, he might then experience another emotional statement that didn't make sense (or feel good) in his cognitive grid. He considered those each like receiving punches in a boxing ring. In his mind, he realized that if he just withstood them, it would produce progress in our relationship. Sometimes humans need to emote and that eruption can often "burn" the people nearby. So as Mike would not run away when getting stung by two testing expressions in a row, his willingness to stay would serve to engender trust. He tells others, "We seldom get to three punches. If Tammy feels like I'm hanging in there with her as she expresses herself, then I don't often have to take three shots."

Standing in and bearing up in a relationship often causes it to grow exponentially. No one wants to feel like he or she is overwhelming to others, or that others aren't strong enough to handle him or her. Again, remember that the emotional age of someone you love might mean that when he wants to communicate his feelings, he might do so like a pre-adolescent – with extreme language and focused on how the rest of the world isn't treating him fairly. So, when interacting with husbands, parents, and friends who are very different from you, think of the three-punch rule next time you feel like you received a little "ding."

Litmus tests

A litmus test is an experiment that "uses a single indicator to prompt a decision."[36] Many people who come into our lives are administering little tests to us to decide something about us. Sheila may dribble a bit of gossip out there to see if you'll "bite." She wants to know if she can trust you with a confidence. Terry may express his political opinion to see if you are safe enough to talk about his sexual struggles. Lakisha might tell you she's had a "horrible past" to see if you care enough to pick up on it and engage her about it. Max could be sharing about his drinking binge last night, closely watching to see if you'll judge him, join in with him, or be the one person with whom he could share his fear that he might be an alcoholic. Adolescents do this all the time. They will tell a friend, teacher, or parent a portion of the truth to see how they react to it. If the response is loving, then they often spill the goods and share the whole truth.

Another definition of litmus test is a "set of questions or exercises evaluating skill or knowledge."[36] We question others to evaluate if they will be people with whom a soul connection might be possible. While most of us do it to some degree or other, these little tests can make or break a person's decision to relate more authentically. Recognizing when others are doing this can be a catalyst for significant movement in a relationship. However, do you know when you yourself are doing it?

Larry Crabb describes how sometimes our conversations are little more than two self-protective styles of relating.[37] The litmus test reality reminds me of his point. Our posturing, probing, and casing the joint of who others are reveals to us again who we ultimately trust in relationship – God or ourselves. Again, litmus tests come back to fear. Right now, will you by faith transfer your relationally sinful patterns to the Lord as He reveals them to you? Will you trust Him enough to have grace for others' litmus tests, and to cease doing your own?

Squishy spots

Another area of relational insight is to be aware that we all have squishy spots. I envision these as weak, extremely tender areas that when "touched" elicit a very strong reaction. That reaction will be disproportionate to the actual situation that triggered it. Have you ever accidentally placed your hand on the shoulder of someone you didn't know had horrible sunburn? He or she will flip out unexpectedly, pulling away from our innocent touch with vigor. When a person goes ballistic over being asked "What do you want for dinner?", that might be evidence of a squishy spot. Someone who corrects you forcefully when you mispronounce her name might be reacting out of one of these spots. Only God really knows why those areas exist, because they are usually a conglomeration of many factors. But however they got there, being aware of when we've touched off another's squishy spot can help us love each other well.

Have you ever looked over only to see someone in a Bible study completely ashen and sweating? Perhaps he heard the verse that someone twisted to condemn him to hell as a child. Maybe you've witnessed a normally extroverted friend shut down in a crowd. I'll never forget sitting with a woman who had a fairly harsh exterior, was highly cognitive, and known to be an opinionated, type-A person. Without warning, tears began to pour from her eyes, and her face transformed into one with a look of fear. Quite literally, nothing had happened. However, a specific word had come up in conversation that caused her to be overcome with pain because it was the very word that shaped her elementary years in a negative direction. Her example reminds us that stepping on another's squishy spot can come without warning.

I had a conversation with someone last week, and she exploded in defensiveness. I was blindsided, but the Lord reminded me I must have stumbled upon a squishy spot. So, I prayed and tried to stay in the conversation rather than getting out of there as fast as I could, which was my natural impulse. Instead, I searched myself for what could have been done to touch this tender area. Of course, it was not the time to calmly ask her, "You seem a little upset. What might have just occurred that is causing this hugely disproportionate reaction to our otherwise pleasant conversation?"! However, in my head I recounted my words, focused in on the topic area, and listened as intently as I could to what she was saying. It's hard to listen to the degree we need to when emotions are mounting, but that is usually a critical time we do so. Not overreacting to another's overreaction is often one of the toughest things to do in a relationship.

When a person's trust has been severed, he might jump all over you if you said you were going to be somewhere and then weren't. A sexual abuse survivor will decompensate into a pile of mush when someone with a strong personality pushes her boundaries. The person whose parents were overly critical will become wildly defensive when asked a simple, "Why did you do that?" innocuously by even a good friend. The person who lived in fear of the next rage-filled blowup by his alcoholic father will be jumpy and perhaps even paranoid around others. I know of a person who literally disappears at times in groups. Suddenly, he will be nowhere to be found. His life when growing up at home was so unpredictable and unsafe that he would hide in closets and corners for hours on end. Present day behavior has identifiable roots. Squishy spots come from somewhere. Understanding this fact allows us to again practice believing the best and looking beyond, as encouraged in previous chapters.

So, the take-away for squishy spots is two-fold: (1) When we realize we have touched another's area of tenderness, it is unwise to engage it. While we should not exit the conversation (even though that might be our natural urge), it is likewise wrong to continue poking at someone's bruise. When you accidentally step on the mine in the field you had no idea was there, don't let it decimate you. Just stop and say "I'm sorry." At that point, the fact that it was unintentional on your part is irrelevant. A quick apology yields more gain than most of us realize. (2) We also need to learn to monitor our own squishy spots. What do I overreact to? How am I too touchy or hypersensitive? When someone detonates one of your hidden explosives, don't take her out for her unwitting misstep.

Don't feed the birds

A particularly tricky area of relationships has to do with giving another person what he or she wants from you, even when it is harmful. I am reminded of the massive goose population found in the surrounding areas where I live. Like gulls at the beach, they will swarm and gorge endlessly when being fed food from humans. It is likely they would continue gluttonously until they explode. Like these geese, there are people who will unknowingly beg from you what you have to offer and not realize what they are trying to get from you is not what they truly desire. (This idea is explained fully in *Soul Healing*, for the interested reader.)

Especially if you are acting in ways that are Christlike, you will be a magnet. As a city on a hill, salt and light, you will be very attractive to a wide variety of people (Matthew 5:14-16). There will be people in your life with whom you will have reciprocal, life-giving, life-long soul connections. There will be others who have no idea that they come to you with a subtle demand. They likewise do not realize you can never provide what would truly quench their thirst.

This concept is extremely difficult to capture in black and white, but if perhaps even one relationship will benefit by this understanding, it is worth our attempt to grasp it. Others might want your affirmation too much. Give it generously, but appropriate to the age and stage of your relationship. Some might want your time in large quantity. Give what you can without compromising the priority of family members and friends in your life. Maybe you have a person who puts you on a pedestal. Maybe you have someone who treats you like a child or second-class citizen in order to make herself feel more powerful, because she knows you won't stand up to her. Be they belittling or idolizing, those people come to you without knowing that they would never stop and say "I'm full." Because of this, they can burn you out. Like the gulls, they would take and take and take from you as long as you would keep giving, until it destroyed them (and probably you in the process).

The "gull" can be someone who takes your power. Every chance he gets, he likes to cause you to feel shame, like you can never measure up. It could be someone who seeks your affirmation. She will look to you for parental-like nurturing endlessly. A person of this type could be using your servant gifting to her benefit without realizing it. You might not see it as such, but her constant crises, cries for help, and need for counsel, while legitimate to some degree, might also be a manipulative tool for getting you to do something for her. If you have a fear of not being able to keep someone at bay, get a sinking feeling when you see a certain number on the caller ID, or feel a sense of dread over the fact that you haven't had lunch with so-and-so in too long, these might be indicators. Such signs can tell you when someone is unwittingly trying to use you to fill a need you can't, and probably shouldn't fulfill.

It is also possible that you yourself are the one who seeks from others that which is not healthy for you. Have you ever wondered why all of your friends are female, if you are a male, or vice versa? Isn't it curious to you how all the people you are around are older than you? Why, do you think, are you attracted to body-builder type males or intellectual females? Have you ever noticed that you really, really care (too much) what opinionated people think? Anytime you are willing to analyze what you are trying to get from people that truly only God can give, it is a good exercise. There are legitimate and illegitimate needs when it comes to what others can meet. To bring your unmet needs to another person is like asking him to pay someone else's bill. Is someone handing you the bill her mother never paid? Are you insidiously slipping your dead brother's balance due statement in someone else's lap? Today in my office, I sat with someone who admitted he was bringing his mother's unpaid bill to his girlfriend, and that even though she loved him well, it just wasn't enough. Only as we come to others with appropriate and healthy expectations will true soul connections occur. Setting others free reaps a fulfilling reward!

The blessing of boundaries

Boundaries is a large discussion all its own. Books, conferences, and groups exist about this topic alone. However, the concept must be mentioned here, because boundaries bring to light some aspects of relational fear. For instance, if you do not have good boundaries, you will be afraid that others will drain you, or just plain make you feel totally crummy about yourself. As well, those with poor boundaries are the ones most open to further hurt and violation. It is devastating how often children abused in childhood are abused in adulthood. Part of this cycle has to do with the lack of knowing what boundaries are and how they work. Therefore, fear is appropriate in this context. The learning point here is that if you are someone who is extremely fearful in relationships, then perhaps you have never understood what boundaries are, how to have them, and how to maintain them.

Emotional and psychological boundaries, as in the physical world, have to do with a sense of "yours" and "mine." Boundaries are what define where you end and I begin. They delineate what is available and open to the public and what is not. When we drive by private land, we clearly know what that means. Stay out. At a college where students are not permitted to walk on the grass, they stay on the sidewalks. Emotionally speaking, when someone you don't know that well asks you about your sex life, that is crossing a boundary. You haven't given him or her permission to enter that area of your life (and if you have, *you* are the one with boundary issues). To take something from another person without asking is a boundary violation. That was hers, and you must ask to have it. Stealing a person's choice about whether to give you something or not is a boundary infringement. Rape is an extreme example. But, speaking on behalf of another person, making an assumption about what she wants to do, breaking a confidence that he has asked you to keep, bringing up something someone shared with you and using it against her – these are all more minor boundary violations that can have a major impact on relationships. Learning about where our own and others' boundaries lie is important to developing soul connections.

When we have appropriate boundaries, we are less likely to self-protect (unless our self-protection is because we are too prideful to let others see our flaws). With boundaries, we can act and react to others in a confident, trusting way, because we have clarity about whom we let into the deeper courtyards of our soul and whom we don't. People who think in extremes tend to think if they open up and let others in, it means they have to immediately let them all the way in. The correct and healthy picture of self in relationship to others is a concentric circle diagram. In the outer circle are those with whom we have minimal contact. The next ring holds acquaintances. Then friends. Then close friends, and dearest friends and family. Taking an inventory and assessing where the people in our life fall, and where they should fall, is a good preparatory boundary exercise. With good boundaries and a heart full of faith in God, you can let go of all fear in relationships!

Flush the fear

When I think of fear, unfortunately, I think of lice. Whenever someone in a home gets lice, the entire place has to be treated – scrubbed completely down in every nook and cranny. Items with too much exposure even have to be burned. Families fighting lice often have it consume their lives for weeks until it is under control. They're so problematic because they're so small, yet invade everywhere. That's like fear. When it comes in, it's really hard to spot, but then before you know it, it has taken over the whole house. Fear grows when not confronted. I once heard that fear and faith cannot coexist. It's true. It's either one or the other. If you have faith, then your trust in God will override fear. If you fear, then you do not trust. Sounds simple, huh?

Well, we all know that fear is such an insidious thing, and that evil is constantly – and I mean constantly – trying to woo us to be afraid. "What if so-and-so thinks you're stupid?" "What if he betrays your trust?" "What if she rejects you?" "What did she mean by that?" "Why didn't they ask us over?" "What if my spouse is lying to me?" Fear in relationships is undoubtedly a huge connection buster. We have to go after it with a vengeance, like using the specialized shampoo for lice. Target it. Identify your own fears and bring them one by one to the Lord. Your relationship with Him is your primary business. Your relationships with others are *His* business. However, most of us think more about, cogitate on, and concern ourselves more with our relationships with others than with Him. We've got it backwards. Press into Him in faith with all your might, and see what He does to your fear in all areas, including your relationships.

We must let go of fear. Yes, even the fear of our own neediness. So many Christians have this particular concept dreadfully backwards. Somehow the church has come to embrace a picture of the "strong Christian" as the smiling, unflappable, never struggling, kids-all-perfect, bastion of godliness and faith at all times. What is that?!? Every person who walks this earth puts his or her pants on one leg at a time, and has issues, struggles, failures, successes, strengths, and weaknesses. Why do you so despise your own weakness? Do you spend your days trying to cover it? Didn't God Himself tell us through Paul that when we feel weak, God's power rests on us? (2 Corinthians 12:10) Again, let us be reminded that our faith is in a God who made us for His purposes and sustains us still. There is nothing you have done to give life to yourself, save yourself from eternal damnation, or make yourself a "good Christian." It's all the work of a benevolent God who sent Christ to be our all-in-all!! Therefore, we must realize our own neediness for what it is, and stop living in fear of it being exposed.

Might I offer a new definition of "needy"? It is allowing the legitimate needs that are there to be a part of your everyday functioning. It does not mean that you will be a bane of burden to everyone around you. It does not mean that you will be a victim. While those are temptations, if you are seeking to put your faith in God for your relationships and exercise the strength of the living Christ available to you, your needs will not overwhelm others. It's when we don't realize that we are trying too often to get strength, purpose, meaning, and love from others that we then become burdensome. They cannot give what only God can. We must embrace the truth about ourselves and others – that much of who we are boils down to the simple fact that we're emotional people.[38] Let's today stop running from our own and others' emotions, for we have a God who will embolden us as He delivers us from whatever fear we face: "I sought the Lord and he answered me and delivered me from all my fears" (Psalm 34:4).

Letting go of fear is a huge component of true soul connections. We abandon our care to God, period. Not only do we trust Him with our temporal lives, we willfully choose to trust Him with our emotional selves. In taking such risks, we paradoxically find the peace we were trying so hard to manipulate and preserve in the first place. The

> "...great paradox is that it is in letting go, we receive. We find safety in unexpected places of risk. And those who try to avoid all risk, those who would try to guarantee that their hearts will not be broken end up in a self-created hell."[39]

Oh, Lord Jesus, that we might follow your example of a steadfast gaze on the goodness of an Almighty Father, rather than on the whims and weaknesses of fallen people.

Chapter Five

LEAN IN

The thrust of this chapter is essentially the action point of the entire book – lean into relationship. Move towards soul connection. Go forward in your desires for better relationships. So much of having better friendships, marriages, and meaningful interchanges is simply a result of the willingness to go further into them. To "lean in" implies action such as taking risks, believing God for what is better, sharing your heart, expressing your feelings, telling someone what he or she means to you, or finding out another's real story. It is to intentionally move towards closeness and connection rather than away from it. Whatever form it takes, to lean in is to "make *every effort* to live in peace with all men and to be holy" (Hebrews 12:14). When we think of all that God purchased for us in Christ and the abundant life that we are to live, the risk to "lean in" seems the least we can do.

What do we do when we see something really unusual? We stare. Our natural inclination is to be fascinated by extreme differences from that which we normally encounter. Certainly, we all have witnessed innocent children who call out "Where is her leg?" or "Look at his green hair!" However, as we get older, it seems we grow into one of two reactions to such stark differences. We either stare as hard as we did when we were children, or we steer clear. I'm disappointed to say, but I did both this afternoon. At my son's soccer game, there was a couple who is quite different from me. I engaged them in conversation, and we had a nice interchange. However, on the way home from that same outing, Mike and I passed a woman who was clearly "off" somehow. I looked away and steered clear. Generally, it seems that when it comes to other humans, we are threatened by difference. How did this come to be, I wondered, given that we all begin with a childlike curiosity?

Prejudice, stereotypes, judgments, preferences, cultural mores and norms – these can barricade us from God's children of all colors and shapes. They rob from us the beauty of being enlarged as people by interacting with others quite different from us. The word of God tells us to love each other deeply (1 Peter 4:8), to live in harmony with one another as brothers (1 Peter 3:8), and to be bound together in perfect unity (Colossians 3:14). The Lord describes us as members of one body – His body – and speaks of how the indispensable parts of the body are those that seem to be weaker (1 Corinthians 12:22). Further, "God has combined the members of the body and has given greater honor to the parts that lacked it, so that *there should be no division in the body,* but that its parts should have equal concern for each other" (1 Corinthians 12:24-25). Differences are from the Lord, specifically designed to manifest His character and Kingdom!

Clearly, instead of running from difference, we are to appreciate it at a minimum and celebrate it at the most. Do you know what people group or types of individuals from whom you keep the most distance? James 2:8-9 has convicting words: "If you really keep the royal law found in Scripture, 'Love your neighbor as yourself,' you are doing right. But *if you show favoritism,* you sin and are convicted by the law as law breakers." God's desire for you and me is that we are free from racial, class, and cultural bias. Instead, we are to realize:

> "...you are no longer foreigners and aliens, but fellow citizens with God's people and members of God's household, built on the foundation of the apostles and prophets, with Christ Jesus himself as the chief cornerstone. In him the whole building is joined together and rises to become a holy temple in the Lord. And in him you too are being built together to become a dwelling in which God lives by His Spirit." (Ephesians 2:19-22)

The bottom line for why we need to lean in to relationship is that we aren't male or female, Jew or Greek, but "are all one in Christ Jesus" (Galatians 3:28).

Dig that

If we are to follow God's way, then we could boil it down to these admonitions:

≈   When you feel the urge to run away from someone, lean in.

≈   When you observe differences in personality, realize these are God's gift to you.

≈   Intentionally pursue diversity in ethnicities, socio-economic brackets, cultures, and personalities.

Have you ever thought about purposefully seeking out friends who are different from you? If you are white, do you have black friends, or vice versa? If you are wealthy, do you closely interact with your blue-collar neighbor? If you are shy, do you have any friends who are loud? Make the change and begin to view all people like we do those at the circus – we enjoy and are fascinated by that which is strange and different. Instead of surrounding yourself with others who look and act like you, force yourself to get around people who intimidate, irritate, and interact in ways that tempt you to withdraw.

There is a line from the movie *Jerry Maguire* that depicts this attitude.[40] Jerry is a white sports consultant and his client Rod is a black football player, striving to break through to the pros. Many of their interactions highlighted their differences, but in one scene, they had a particularly intense interaction. When Rod was completely imitating and mocking a rant Jerry gave, he suddenly got serious and said, "And I *dig* that about you!" Can we become people who might not understand why someone is the way he or she is, but who can have the attitude that we "dig" unique personalities? Who is God bringing to your mind as you read this?

It is so neat how God will underscore to me the very point about which I am writing at the time of writing it. Literally, just this morning, one of our neighbor's parents came walking towards our house after hearing my son's motorcycle. He had on a long white tunic with baggy white pants and a pair of tan sandals. His brown skin and thick eyebrows were prominent in contrast to his linen garb. We had never met before, but to hear his heavy accent was so refreshing to me. I now have on my counter a post-it note with Rami Koshtas's address and phone number because he wants us to call him when we remember the name of a motorcycle shop. How fun is that?

When we lose our inhibitions and practice an open, non-threatened stance towards others, it truly is exciting. For many years in my thirties, I had a birthday party with 20 or so friends and we would do a variety of fun activities, but the staple was laser tag. It was always hilarious to watch people's personalities completely morph upon entering that smoky arena. The true beauty, though, was seeing the diversity of women running, hiding, shooting, and even crawling. Our ages spanned from 25 to 59, our physiques from tiny to big, our personalities from quiet to loud, and none of that mattered. Something during that time spoke to my soul as a feeling of "this is how it is meant to be." God created us all vastly different on purpose – to display His character in our diversity!

The real deal

Another way to lean into relationship and move into an all-around more God-glorifying life is confirmed by secular research.[41] Studies have shown that self-disclosure begets self-disclosure. In other words, if one party will take the lead in connective conversation and open up to share some personal revelation, the odds of the other party or parties doing so become very high. Practically speaking, if you want someone to open up more, then open up yourself. To share a dream, a fear, a failure, a success, a feeling…anything can be a disclosure

Self-disclosure begets self-disclosure.

if it comes from the true core of a person and isn't part of everyday conversation.

Years ago, a friend of mine and I were talking. We got really honest at one point, and shared our fears about being each other's friend. Although we had been good friends, I never shared the shame of my life with him, because I knew of his internal (judgmental) reaction to people who struggled with what I did. When I told him this, he began to cry, joining with the tears of vulnerability I had been shedding. And I'll never forget what he said next because it captures the true essence of honest human connection. He looked at me and said, "Now this is where it gets real and good, doesn't it? This is the good stuff." Mind you, I was sharing the shame of my life and calling him out for being judgmental. It wasn't a fluffy feel-good moment.

What it was, though, was two fallen human beings sharing with unedited honesty about areas of weakness and failure. In that moment, there was a beauty. I would have to call it the "yes" of the Holy Spirit, which I believe happens when we find ourselves in places and situations that cause us to say, "I was meant for this." I knew my friend was experiencing the same reality. He was right. It was indeed a beautiful moment of the "good stuff" as we thrust ourselves into a deeper level of exposure and resultant dependence upon God. Self-disclosure begets a deeper level of friendship and connection that is reciprocated most of the time.

Of course, I must offer a caveat at this point. I am not proposing that you become a person who shares a great deal with the wrong people. Individuals who self-disclose too much, too early, or too often end up alienating others. They appear self- absorbed. If you tend to be a "talker," "inappropriate," or one who "wears your heart on your sleeve," then this section is not wholly applicable to you. For you, to concentrate on listening, looking beyond, and loving like the big one would be the better foci. However, for most people who live self-protectively or in fear, the advice to lean in through self-disclosure could be life-changing. A character from *Catcher in the Rye* illustrates the blessing of this truth in tongue-in-cheek fashion: "Don't ever tell anybody anything. If you do, you start missing everybody."[42] Vulnerability promotes close relationship.

Get over it

Sometimes in parenting, mothers and fathers have the perspective, "You have no idea what you need, but I do" when it comes to their children. Taken with a grain of salt, this is what I am encouraging for the "lean in" posture to occur. In other words, even if a person seems resistant to your overtures for connection, he or she longs for relationship. As we belabored in the first section of this book, there is not one human being who doesn't desire to be connected with others. This is true whether he or she acknowledges it or not.

So, with this as the backdrop, I believe you should think of yourself as the "press in," "move-the-conversation-to-authentic-places" leader, period. Act like that parent who knows what's best for the child. Just do it because you actually do know it is best. Don't be a relationship chicken any longer, and lean in! Admittedly, there is a fine line between leading others well and violating personal boundaries. If you are moving toward another with love for him or her in focus, you will be able to read these signs. If, however, you are pressing in out of some personal agenda, then you may unintentionally end up hurting someone. "Lean in" happens through a delicate intertwining of leadership and sensitivity.

Another example of this tenuous balance between leadership and sensitivity is touch. My answer to the question of "To touch or not to touch?" is a resounding "yes!" The impact of human physical contact cannot be measured. It

113

saves people's lives, changes their outlooks, calms their fears, comforts their hurts, and enlivens their strength. Some people will do anything for a hug, and I mean anything. I knew a person who would have sex simply for the few moments of nonsexual hugging. How sad, but true. I touch people constantly – shaking hands, touching shoulders, hugging – and the impact has been so profound as to be overwhelming. People are starving for it. Giving appropriate, nonsexual hugs, handshakes, and touches can literally change a person's belief in him or herself as loveable, likeable, or even valuable. We don't touch what disgusts us. Human touch imparts value.

However, because of how advertisers attempt to hypnotize us to over-sexualize everything, it is crucial that you understand what appropriate and inappropriate touch is. True soul connection happens when these boundaries are clear. If not, you could unwittingly be leading a brother or sister into temptation. For example, women, you must be aware of where your chest is when you are hugging a male friend. I recommend the A-frame hug, which is like an A-frame house, connected at the top, but with space between the bodies from the shoulders down. Men, you cannot talk near a woman's ear when you are giving her a hug. Ladies, touching a man with your feet is not wise when you are not married to him. Gentlemen, touching a woman on the small of her back is not as appropriate as between her shoulder blades or on her shoulder. These subtleties are important and instructive. Most importantly, though, is that you are constantly monitoring your own motives when it comes to touch. If your heart is in the right place, others will sense that and not misinterpret your kindness.

So, the message of the "lean in" admonition here is simple. Instead of hiding behind some thickly erected emotional barrier, put yourself out there. You are God's man or woman! He needs you in the forceful advancement of His loving kingdom plan. Instead of running away, run toward. Rather than disengaging when someone seems weird, engage. When encountering someone very different from yourself, embrace the difference. Realize this could very well be part of God's plan for expanding you and growing you up. Let go of anything that gets in your way, and "as God's chosen people, holy and dearly loved, clothe yourselves with compassion, kindness, humility, gentleness, and patience" (Colossians 3:12). We "lean in" by looking beyond, loving big, listening long, letting go of fear, and as we shall see next, losing the black robe of judgment.

Chapter Six
LOSE THE BLACK ROBE

It's no coincidence that judges wear black robes. Or that Darth Vader does, for that matter. Robes are associated with power. The color black is associated with finality. Judges most certainly have tremendous power to decide a person's fate. The damage of figuratively donning a black robe in a friendship is severe. Years of a beautiful relationship can be devastated by one errant comment filled with judgment. It's a biblical admonition to beware of judgmentalism:

> "Anyone who speaks against his brother or judges him speaks against the law and judges it. When you judge the law, you are not keeping it, but sitting in judgment on it. There is only one Lawgiver and Judge, the one who is able to save and destroy. But you – who are you to judge your neighbor?" (James 4:11-12)

Really, what makes us think we have any right to judge another? We believers know God's promise that each person will be held accountable for what he or she has done in this life, so why do we take it upon ourselves to evaluate anyone? Romans 14:10 gives it to us point blank: "You, then, why do you judge your brother? Or why do you look down on your brother? For we will all stand before God's judgment seat."

A look in the mirror

When we judge others, we are not displaying Jesus. He did not cast a stone at the woman caught in adultery, but told her to go and sin no more (John 8:11). He did not steer clear of the maligned tax collector, but invited him down for a chat (Luke 19:2). He did not disassociate from prostitutes or lepers, but celebrated life with them.[43] Jesus' own words to His followers were as clear on the subject as were His actions. "Do not judge, or you too will be judged. For in the same way you judge others, you will be judged and with the measure you use, it will be measured you" (Matthew 7:1-2). Isn't that a daunting thought – that we will be assessed by the same standard we apply to others? When you think disapproving thoughts of the mother who is yelling at her child in the parking lot, are you forgetting that you did the same in the car on the way to school? Just because you would never be caught dead yelling in public doesn't excuse your anger.

It's as if Jesus is telling us not to give others our personal "do's and don'ts" list. If you are convicted to recycle or to drive the speed limit or never to drink alcohol or to vote Republican, that doesn't mean others who don't hold such beliefs are going to hell. While we are certainly admonished to stand by our convictions (Joshua 22:5), we are not told to bash these beliefs over others' heads. Being judgmental is like wielding a bludgeoning instrument. The hit is strong, broad, and damaging, sometimes beyond repair. It is a dangerous entity with daunting consequences. The point here is that we are, for all intents and purposes, just plain foolish if we are willing to sit as judge in another's life.

"You, therefore, have no excuse, you who pass judgment on someone else, for at whatever point you judge the other, you are condemning yourself, because you who pass judgment do the same things. Now we know that God's judgment against those who do such things is based on truth. So when you, a mere man, pass judgment on them and yet do the same things, do you think you will escape God's judgment?" (Romans 2:1-3).

Reality is that we usually struggle most with people most like us. If you judge prideful people, you most likely have a blind spot of pride. If you find yourself condemning those with lots of money, you probably have issues with money. If you internally sneer at someone who is often the center of attention, you are envious of what he or she has. And the kicker is that if we are irritated with judgmental people, it's because we've judged them first.

Certainly, we are to make assessments about situations and even people, but *to be judgmental is very different from being discerning.* We are indeed to identify those who are weaker brothers, ones caught in sin, and who are timid, for example (Romans 14, 15; Galatians 6:1; 1 Thessalonians 5:14). However, we are to be sensitive to them, seek to gently restore them, and encourage them, respectively. Nowhere is the discernment gift given as license to use godly assessments in ungodly ways. To whom much is given, much is required, says God's Word (Luke 12:48). If you have been given the tremendous gift of discernment, more is required from you than to slap personal labels or diatribes on someone about whom God has given you insight.

Since you are still reading at this point, I feel confident you are not, nor would you ever think about, being overtly judgmental. You hide it well, perhaps even from yourself. But behavior is not what is in question here. It is all about how each one handles this in his own mind. We're talking about the heart. What is in your heart towards your difficult father-in-law, your meddlesome neighbor, your narcissistic sister, or your overbearing boss? Are you willing to honestly entertain the reality that it's not *if* you are judgmental, but who you are judging and how you are judging them? Such a posture will not only honor God, but will permit us a look in the mirror to see how we are guilty of the very things we critique in others.

Freed from my positions, preferences, and practices

Living in such a way as to leave all judgment (again, not discernment) to God means we realize that others have no reason at all to agree with our personal preferences, positions, and practices. It also means that we live like God is the only judge. We don't slander another because he or she didn't choose to do things exactly how we would. Instead, we daily recall the grace and mercy that God has shown to us, and we extend it to others in the same manner He does to us – *freely*. This is what it means to live by grace. It is one thing to have access to God's grace; it is another thing to extend it to others. In other words, God's grace is always available to you and me as children of God, but we must *choose* to give it to others. To offer the grace of God to others is a willful, intentional, on-purpose decision.

One of the most challenging times to give others grace and refrain from judgmentalism is when others hold dissimilar positions from ours. Historically, those claiming the name of Christ have judged, accused, and even executed those with differing opinions. Eighteenth-century theologian Matthew Henry reminded the church, "It is contrary to the law of justice, as well as charity, to censure those who differ in opinion from us as transgressors."[44] Perhaps the way you read the Bible makes it impossible for you to see the issue of baptism, or tongues, or women's roles any differently than you do. When we do encounter this situation, Crabb says, "Our sinful tendency is rather to quietly and unconsciously enjoy criticizing a position different from ours. We shake our heads in sad regret over our brother's error while our hearts beat with the happy excitement of felt superiority."[45] Kay Arthur offers this perspective:

> "Have you noticed that many of our conflicts with other believers involve judging one another in the gray area of do's and don'ts, and differences, all depending on our religious upbringing or lack of it? How I pray we will take to heart the words of the apostle Paul: 'Who are you to judge the servant of another? To his own master he stands or falls; and he will stand, for the Lord is able to make him stand' (Romans 14:4). We need to remember that when we walk according to love and 'pursue the things which make for peace and the building up of one another' (Romans 14:19), then we need not worry about wrongfully passing judgment. Are you sitting as judge rather than walking in love toward your brother? Are you seeking to judge the motives of people's hearts when you can only see their outward appearance? Have you, like the Pharisees, added your traditions to God's Word

and then sought to judge another individual's walk with God according to your interpretation of the Law?"[46]

Our positions, and even our preferences, are simply that – *ours*. Even if they are held because of a strong conviction from the Lord, you are still not permitted to judge another as less spiritual, less mature, less committed than you if they do not hold the same ideals and ideas.

Likewise, we trip up in the area of becoming judgmental when we think what has worked for us will surely work for others. It can begin very innocently, or even kindheartedly. Someone asks us for advice or our opinion, and we give it. We are excited to share how a certain plan or program or approach has been a godsend in our lives. The problem occurs, though, when he or she doesn't take our suggestion. So often, we slip into judgmentalism. Accidental offense occurs when we assume that what has been a huge success in our lives will most certainly be the answer for others' very similar problems. Even great ideas for having devotions, staying organized, raising children, losing weight, improving your marriage, or managing finances can become ways in which we judge others if we are not careful.

When God has seemingly opened our eyes to His plan for us in a particular area, we are especially vulnerable to assuming this is God's will for others. I had someone specifically come to my house to tell me I would be out of God's will if I didn't use the Bradley method for childbirth. (She never thought to first ask me what our plan was.) I've seen Christian parents judge others over views on birth control, potty training, teaching children to read, and when to feed infants. I've observed friendships end over vitamin supplements, approaches to home management, and financial priorities. I've known of church members who divided over musical preferences, worship styles, foyer colors, and the children's curriculum. *How can this be?!?*

> "I care very little if I am judged by you or by any human court; indeed, I do not even judge myself...It is the Lord who judges me. Therefore, judge nothing before the appointed time; wait till the Lord comes. He will bring to light what is hidden in darkness and will expose the motives of men's hearts. At that time, each will receive his praise from God." (1 Corinthians 4:3-5)

We will all answer to God for our judgments of others.

Faulty vision

When we set ourselves up as judge of another's life, we are essentially saying that we understand the situation. It implies that we can see all the facts and are therefore equipped to conclude what is going on and what another should do about it. But, we never have all the facts. The only way humans can judge is by looking at externals. John 7:24 records, "Stop judging by mere appearances, and make a right judgment," which implies that judging by externals leads to wrong conclusions.

Instead, we are to view others in the faith through spiritual eyes. We are to see them as they are in Christ, which is as brand-new creatures whose sins have been forgiven (Colossians 2:13, 1 John 2:12). Paul exhorts, "Therefore from now on we recognize no one according to the flesh...if anyone is in Christ, he is a new creature; the old things passed away; behold, new things have come" (2 Corinthians 5:16-17). This fantastic news for us is that because of Christ, our past is not held against us. Can we not extend just a portion of that grace to others? Don't hold a "past" against anyone whom God in His great mercy has redeemed. Would you make yourself greater than God?

Freed from being the Holy Spirit

When I teach at women's conferences in particular, I always receive a knowing laugh when I remind women that they are not their husbands' Holy Spirit. Although I personally can't identify at all with this, it seems that women sometimes feel the necessity to prompt, guide, direct, and yes, even convict their *We are not each other's Holy Spirit.* husbands. (Okay, maybe I can identify a little.) However, the truth is that the Holy Spirit is others' Holy Spirit. Whether it is a spouse, a friend, a neighbor, or even a person in your church, we are not each other's Holy Spirit. Our insistence on "helping" the Holy Spirit along in the lives of our loved ones is actually interference, luring their attentions towards our desires and diverting it from the press of God's Spirit. Therefore, we are relieved from being the keeper of all that is right and good (in our opinion) for those around us. We instead know that the Lord is perfectly capable of directing others' lives.

We cannot, nor should we, be another's conscience. It's our job to accept others, pray for them, and speak truth to them in love (Romans 14:1, Romans 15:7, James 5:16, Ephesians 4:15). It's God's job to direct them, mature them, and refine them. Perhaps our judgmentalism will cease entirely as we realize how ludicrous it is to act like another's Holy Spirit. How about we just pray to God that He will do all He wants in the lives of those close to us? That's living out the reality that the Holy Spirit is active. He's actually more active than we can imagine in our finite minds (Ephesians 3:20). So, let's cease this day from putting others under constraints, condemnation, or conditional love until they "shape up" in Jesus. Let's leave His job to Him.

Antidotes to the poison of judgment

It is not an overstatement to say that hurtful judgmentalism kills. How many lives have been destroyed over something terrible someone said to them when they were young? There are adults walking around who have never gotten over those things. Likewise, how many believers excited about God and church in their newfound faith, have subsequently walked away from church because of the judgmentalism of people? I have more than one person popping into my head as I write this. How about you? What a heartbreak – God saves them and His people alienate them. Now, I know that sounds dramatic, and it is certainly not the case the majority of the time, but don't you agree with me that if it happens once, it's happened too much?

The fundamental antidote to the disease of judgmentalism is simply to stay close to the Lord Jesus. If you are regularly confessing your own sin, the apparent sins of others will seem minimal. If you consider that, apart from God's great mercy, you are deserving of hell, it's not so hard to offer such mercy to another poor human being. If you are in the Word, you will hear over and over the call to love and command to forgive, and will find it more difficult to judge others with His Word ringing in your ears. However, if you are straying from the Lord, having stretches of time with no exposure to His Word, or out of fellowship, don't be surprised if you find judgmentalism creeping in very quickly. It is one of hell's favorite things to entice believers to do. Why? Precisely because it's so deadly.

However, there are two practical suggestions to help curb a judgmental spirit. In addition to a steady, strong relationship with Christ, two ways to fight judgmentalism are: (1) focusing on what is instead of what isn't and (2) cultivating empathy. Both involve choosing a shift in perspective. At the moment you are tempted to judge, look at the very disgrace you yourself are committing

The hardest time to see ourselves is when we are judging others.

right then. Really, the hardest time to see ourselves is when we are in the middle of judging others. Two interesting things happened in my son's soccer game last night. First, I was writing this chapter as I was disgusted by the behavior of the opposing team's parents. We had played them in a recent tournament, and one particular red-haired mother was berating the ref, screaming about all the ways in which our players were fouling, and was blinded to the similar play of her own child. Did you catch that? I was actually writing this chapter on judgment as I was judging her. Precious, I know. Thankfully, the Lord brought this to my mind as I sat in my Coleman chair, and I repented right then and there. Her offensiveness was obvious, but mine...insidious.

Secondly, my son Shaeffer was on offense, and a boy was defending him. He took a strong tumble, and the ref blew the whistle for an in-the-box penalty kick. Those of you who know soccer know that such a call means a good chance of a goal. However, Shay looked up and said, "No, I just fell. I tripped." Not only did the ref look stunned, so were the parents on the sideline. A nine-year-old volunteering the truth, which could decide the outcome of the game? This is a competitive soccer league. This is why the movie "Kicking and Screaming" was made in the first place. Didn't Shay know how massively important in the span of life this game was?!?! In all seriousness, what happened was that play went on, the call was reversed, and the game ended in a tie. But, the parents were impacted. The reason? Because before they could hear what Shaeffer was doing, they were screaming, "He was *not* fouled! Come on, ref! Are you blind?!" In the midst of delivering diatribes on the innocent ref, they missed how ridiculous their irate judgment looked as a nine-year-old appeared to be the most mature person around. When we are judging others, we have a very hard time seeing ourselves. Our focus can't be on two places at one time. You are either judging another or seeing yourself. A key to becoming less judgmental in life is keeping our eyes on ourselves and our own sinfulness.

Another such shift in perspective is focusing on what *is* rather than what *is not*. Such a change can be life-altering. Myriad marriages are destroyed by spouses who focus only on what their mates do not do or provide or offer, rather than what they do. People leave churches in droves because they spotlight what the church is not doing, rather than how it does function. Friendships falter due to how the other person is not a good friend, rather than how he or she is a true friend. Nothing on this earth is ever perfect, especially humans. Therefore, there will always be something dissatisfying or disturbing about everyone and everything. If you are someone who focuses on what is not, you will never find joy. You will bemoan how you don't have a house like so-and-so's rather than being thankful for the one you do have. You will look at the faults of your children over their strengths. You will focus on what is not good about your marriage, or family, or job, rather than what is good about them – or that you even have them in the first place!

Shifting our vantage point to *what is* will not only impact us deeply, it will also help keep us from judgmentalism. We will focus on how someone is uniquely made in the image of God rather than how irritating or immature he or she is. We'll celebrate that we do have enough money to see a movie rather than complain about how we don't have enough to see a concert. We'll be thankful for the crying baby we do hold in our arms rather than the deafening silence the infertile couple down the street must endure. We will see how our child's argumentativeness is a strength, our friend's forgetfulness is the other side of why she's so forgiving of us, and our mother-in-law's distance from our children means she doesn't meddle in how we raise them. If we can train our minds to focus on what *is* good or right or unique about a person, rather than what is lacking in him or her, judgmentalism fades into grey.

Finally, empathy is also a key to battle being judgmental. While much has been written on it in both secular and Christian literature, it all boils down to this: putting yourself in another's shoes. Empathy has to do with concentrating not on what *you* think about someone's life, but what *he* thinks about his life. You imagine what it must be like to be him, with his job, kids, and wife, and how he must feel in life. You empathize with someone by really concentrating on how she could reach a certain conclusion or have hurt feelings, rather than what your personal thoughts about the situation are.

As empathy comes from *em pathos*, which literally means "to feel into," you train yourself to literally enter the world of another, suspending your own personality, strengths, and experience.[47] The power of looking to understand another's point of view, feelings, and perceptions cannot be underestimated. The next time you pick up a phone call from a friend, mentally tell yourself that your priority for this conversation is to clearly grasp the other's world. It changes the entire exchange. Empathy is a beautiful tool which honestly is a key to negotiating all of life, but especially relationships. Most successful leaders have developed a capacity for empathy. If we can learn to put ourselves in others' shoes, then we are less apt to make negative sweeping assessments of others or what they do.

True soul connection is sabotaged, if not completely prohibited, by the presence of judgmentalism. If you desire relationships with others that are fulfilling, you must be willing to put your own haughty assessments aside. To sincerely join with a person, you realize you never know the entirety of any situation, let alone any person. You choose instead to focus on who they are, not your personal opinion of them, and to highlight their excellent qualities in your mind. You don't ignore insights about them, but rather extend the grace of God given you over and above their faults. If you long to have friends that really feel like friends, you must refuse to sit in judgment, and instead, give it over to the One who commands we leave them to Him in the first place.

Chapter Seven
LASH OUT AT COMPARISON

Not only is judgment a surefire way to shut down quality relationships, so is comparison. It is a saboteur in every way possible. I love God's Word to this point. Second Corinthians 10:12 states plainly, "They measure themselves with themselves and compare themselves with themselves. They are not wise." Think about how that would be translated in today's language. Something like, "When you compare and measure, you're stupid!" "They are not wise" can't get much more straightforward. So, if you wisely want to have better relationships, comparison can't be a part of those.

To assess who we are or what we have, based on another, is deeply ingrained in our culture. Every commercial, ad, and marketing scheme is designed to get us to look at what we have and decide it is not good enough. It's so entrenched that we don't even realize the extent to which we do it. Therefore, we have to resolutely *refuse* to do it. We'll have to actually fight against it. Think about the things we compare on a daily basis: our bodies, clothes, houses, jobs, children, cars, spouses, churches, friends, purses, talents, and on and on ad nauseam. Why is it so dangerous? What makes it so "unwise," as Scripture suggests?

We need only look at the results of comparison to see its toxicity. When someone contrasts himself against another, usually one of two outcomes occurs. Either he assesses himself as somehow better than another, engendering pride, or he evaluates that he is not as good as someone else. When we compare ourselves with others, most often the result is discontentment – with others, with possessions, with circumstances. Jealousy, dissatisfaction, and judgment are just a few of the by-products of setting yourself up in some side-by-side contest. The question is: does comparison ever lead anywhere good?

Evil has a heyday when believers compare their gifts, abilities, and positions – especially in the church. Sometimes we are so engrossed over using our particular spiritual gift, that we become quickly dissatisfied if we are not. This intensifies especially if we see someone else getting to express his or her gifts. God wants us to have an appreciation for our own and others' roles in the body of Christ. Instead, comparison can create competition and generate spiritual pride. Rather than celebrating when someone is used by God to teach, sing, lead, pray, or hold office in the church, Christians who aren't aware of their comparison issues will find themselves judging and envying others. A. W. Tozer said, "Stop trying to compete with others. Give yourself to God and then be who you are, without regard to what others think."

The reaction of envying another's spiritual gift can lead to discouragement, even contempt, towards one's own gifting. My friend, Drew, who has the gift of mercy, relates, "I've struggled to feel that I have a valuable place in the body since I am not good at teaching or leading a ministry. I wish I had the gifts that really make a difference in the church."

While it's true that some gifts are more public in their effect, every spiritual gift is bestowed to "make a difference"! If Andy hides his gift, who is there to care deeply, pray steadfastly, and have a ministry of presence when a brother in the Lord suffers or falls into sin? Spiritual gifts were not given to make us feel valued or useful. They exist to bless and build up the body of Christ – our fellow believers. (Eph. 4:11-16) Envy and judgmentalism are the polar opposites of our command to "do whatever leads to peace and mutual edification" and to "build each other up" (Romans 14:19, 1 Thessalonians 5:11). The result of comparison is usually sin; hence it really is a stupid thing to do.

Ever since the Garden

Soul connection is made possible by the absence of comparison. However, when someone is caught in the comparison trap, he or she will most likely become discontent, which leads to dissatisfaction. But, an overriding truth for us all is found in John Piper's premise: *God is most glorified in us when we are most satisfied in Him.*[48] Conversely, whatever leads us to dissatisfaction is not glorifying to God. Saying it again, comparison leads to dissatisfaction. Here's the route I'm describing:

> Self/other comparison → discontentment with another, self, or what self has → dissatisfaction with self and other

It's as if comparison is the first domino to fall in a progression straight to the pit of hell.

Okay, I know that is a bit dramatic, but dissatisfaction is hellish. To be disgruntled with the very God who gave you the breath you just took, the eyes to read these words, and the gift of eternal salvation is an affront to Him. I can't help but think of the Garden here. Adam and Eve had everything, and I mean *everything*. Can you possibly imagine being naked and not ashamed?! That's what I'm talking about – a world we can't even imagine. Their souls were at rest in authentic, open communion with one another and God. No hiding was necessary from either God or the other human, because there was no fear. It was amazing – all that our relationships were intended to be. Openness, vulnerability, acceptance, celebration of beauty, complete provision, the comfort of being known, no "secret life," no embarrassing habits or quirks. Fully satisfied.

So, what happened? Evil came alongside Eve and pointed out the one and only thing to which she did not have access. While every possible provision, delight, and enjoyment was hers, there was only one tiny little off-limits space. The serpent swayed her to affix her gaze on that which she could not have. And the rest is literally history. That hellish equation that worked back then still works today. If the forces of hell can tempt us to turn our eyes off God's tremendous provision toward what we don't have – then we falter every time.

Because discontent is so rampant in our society, we don't even realize the degree to which we are falling for this diabolical ploy. Can't you hear it? "Yeah, your husband might be a good provider and dad, but he doesn't meet your emotional needs." "Sure, Sandy was there for you when you had your first baby, but why doesn't she reach out to you more? You're always the initiator." "Your kids get good grades, but the Francis children get good grades *and* play varsity sports." "Pastor Joe is a great preacher and all, but he didn't visit me in the hospital, so the card he sent doesn't really mean a thing."

Sounds pretty wicked, doesn't it? Satan, your flesh, and the world constantly suggest that we doubt God's goodness. It's just so hard to discern because there's always a modicum of truth in the lies that successfully wrap themselves around us. However, this bit of truth must not keep us from rejecting the lie.

The tidbit of truth dupes us into allowing access if we are not resolute to reject the lie. When extra tasks arise in our family life, the responsibility often becomes mine rather than my husband's. Then I am confronted with the thought, "Why do I always have to do all the extra work?!!" When I allow this thought to lodge in my heart, the comparison between the effort I must expend, in comparison with my husband's effort ("Which sport is he watching now?") becomes a seed of bitterness. To refute the untruth, I must remind myself of ways he has been sharing the family load. "Yes, I did cook dinner for guests tonight and now I am cleaning up by myself, but he has been handling the unexpected repairs for both of our cars this week."

Contented, not comparing

While this might seem like a bit of a tangent from how to have soul connections, it really isn't. *If our own soul is never satisfied, no relationship will ever meet our standards.* Honestly, if you are not content in your own soul, you will never experience peaceful,

Dissatisfaction in the soul leads to dissappointing relationships

positive, mutual relationships. We can't get satisfaction from others that we will only be able to find in God. It's like trying to get milk from a pansy. Hard as we try, and beautiful as that flower is, it cannot nourish us. It can delight us, bring us beauty, make us happy and uplifted, but it cannot substitute for fundamental nourishment. It's the same with quality relationships. While they will bring us many nourishing elements – connection, comfort, support, empathy, encouragement – they can never be the foundational bare-boned place of sustenance. Only God can do that. He and His Word are called the bread of life for a reason. Soul connections with others will bring extra nutrition to our soul, but they cannot take the place of a personal relationship with Jesus Christ wherein He alone is the source of satisfaction.

Avoid like the plague

The intentional ploy to woo Christians to be discontent is why I personally don't go to shopping malls. While I certainly would never place that limitation on others, I find that shopping venues are breeding grounds for discontentment. They are comparison-brewing factories designed to produce dissatisfaction in every wallet-carrier who enters. Virtually no one leaves a mall focusing on the Lord, let alone pleased with who He made her to be and what she has. How is evil working against your relationship with the Lord to cause you to focus on what you are unhappy about? How are you tempted to compare? In what ways are you ignoring God's blessing and provision, discounting it in light of what you see another person enjoying? Your soul was made for so much more. Can we this day understand the depth of damage done by comparison and refuse to be caught in that hurtful web any longer?

The definitions of "comparison" include "a statement or estimate of similarities and differences" and "relative estimate." A synonym is "evaluation."[49] These all encompass the idea of making a judgment. As we discovered in the last chapter, judgments by humans quickly lead to judgmentalism, which is forbidden by a God who reserves the right to evaluate His own creation. Comparison is dangerous for the same reason judgment is. At their root, they lead to a questioning of God's sovereignty and an elevation of man's finite perspective. Comparison raises the material over the spiritual. Judgments are made based on the external, not the internal. God's Word is full of warnings that these are saboteurs of His way. The kinds of relationships we yearn for are vanquished if comparison is a part of them. No matter what conclusion is reached through comparative evaluations, the mere process of measuring one human against another taints the potential for true, quality relationships.

Chapter Eight
LASSO YOUR SPEECH

The power of speech cannot be overestimated. God spoke, and all that is came into existence. Jesus Christ is referred to as the Living Word (Revelation 19:13, John 1:1, 14). The Bible is the Word of God (2 Timothy 3:15-17). As discussed in chapter two, an errant word can scar us forever, or a word spoken in love can embolden us with confidence. Words are the primary means humans use to hurt or heal, bless or curse, love or hate. The Bible actually says that what comes out of our mouths has the power of life and death (Proverbs 18:21). *The power of life and death!* Therefore, it is obvious that speech plays a vital part in having superior, life-altering relationships. If we can get control of what comes out of our mouths, we harness one of the most powerful instruments on the face of the earth. The parental warning to "watch your language" takes on new meaning as we consider how to connect our souls with others.

Truer by the minute

Researchers have also seen how powerful speech is. What they have discovered is that the more you verbalize something, the more you believe it, and the truer it becomes. The term "self-fulfilling prophecy" captures this idea. It is the theory that the stronger we perceive a concept in our minds, it will increasingly become our reality. Researchers have found that what we picture and speak actually becomes so. It's as if there's an intangible reality that the more we speak something, the more it actually becomes real. How this happens in a self-fulfilling prophecy is that: (1) we form certain expectations, (2) we communicate those expectations with various unconscious cues, (3) people tend to respond to these cues by adjusting to match them, and (4) the result is that the original expectations become true.[50] I wonder how much God's Word points to this in the verse, "As a man thinks, so he is" (Proverbs 23:7)?[51] If you keep wondering if you will get sick, you most likely will. Talking a lot about how depressed something makes you actually causes you to become depressed. Multiple studies have shown this to be true.[52]

One author hones in on the self-fulfilling prophecy and says we ought to be very careful how we speak. "The more you speak negatively about something, the more that negative statement becomes your point of view. That area of our lives then becomes consistent with the way we say it is."[53] His recommendation is to look at the areas of our lives that aren't working very well right now and notice how we are talking about them. What do you see when you do this? How often do you think you need to verbalize that your child is out of control before he or she will act accordingly? What number of times do you need to mention your spouse's lack of thoughtful actions before he or she ceases to be thoughtful? Simply put, we cannot underestimate the power inherent in our speech.

When we speak negatively about something, we not only lose our own power, we often agree with some hellish suggestion. Remember that evil is constantly trying to get us to buy into lies.[54] Oftentimes, when we talk negatively about ourselves or others, we are actually agreeing with some evil idea that has little to no basis of truth. However, because of the power of speech, the more we speak it, the more it seems true. So, don't say ungodly or ugly things unless you want what you say to be true. Instead, focus on the converse potential in this truth. We can actually cause something to become so by our speaking of it. Certainly, I'm not saying you can become a multimillionaire by just saying it over and over. However, the shaping potential of our words can *never* be underestimated. This is especially true as it relates to other people.[55]

To have real soul connections with others, put into practice choosing your language carefully. Intentionally encourage a person where he or she is weak. Or speak future-focused things like, "I'm sure we'll be friends for a long time," or joining words such as, "We've been through enough already that we certainly can trust each other." Picture in your head what you want that relationship to be like, and then speak as if it is so. For example, "I know I could call you if I really needed help" is one such statement. You are speaking something that might not be entirely the case at present, but that you envision as you think about the kind of relationship you want to have. Stop for a moment and consider the arenas and relationships in which your shaping words could have a major impact. In your relationship with your husband or wife? Your children? A co-worker? Church friend? Really, the potential for speaking something into existence follows the example of the God who made us and His Spirit who now lives in us, if we have accepted Christ.

Speak it how you want it to be and by faith believe that it can be. I often say things such as, "How's the best husband in the world?" or "I can't believe I get to have a child like you" to Mike and our boys. I'll tell Mike that there's no one on earth I'd rather be married to than him. And guess what? True to how the human psyche works, my feelings follow. I honestly can't believe I get to be married to the best man there is. Do you know that this is how it really works? If we align ourselves with some godly truth *regardless of how we feel about it at a particular moment*, over time our feelings actually do change in response to the continued reaffirmation of the godly truth. Feelings come and go, but truth remains. If that which we speak becomes more our reality, then which should we be speaking more – our feelings or some godly truth?

To the boys, I will speak forward-directed hopes like, "We are so blessed to be in this family together. We are going to be close for the rest of our lives." Some days, and especially when the boys are sniping at each other, I'll encourage them to say, "You're a great brother and my best friend." It's fine if the feelings aren't there at a particular moment when you speak something! It's the truth that the other is a great brother, and they actually are each other's best friend. If you want a romantic husband, speak that as a reality rather than criticize his present failure, as is usually the case. Say "Your thought-fulness makes me feel so loved" or "Isn't this wonderful that while other marriages are falling apart, we are falling more in love than ever?" Honestly, can you imagine how impactful, encouraging, and empowering uttering such godly affirmations will be? Start today!

Remember, the power of our speech to shape reality is huge. This isn't some gimmick or psychological head game, but the use of one of the most powerful forces we have on earth. How it works is intangible and immeasurable. That's why it's so hard to see it and grasp it. Again, I say to simply recall some of the most hurtful and most wonderful things people have said to you. Think about how you have developed as you continued hearing those words about yourself in the same manner. If you aren't paying attention, the suggestion someone else made about you gets repeated over and over in your head to the point that before long, you hear it in your own voice and not that person's anymore. It changed from someone else speaking it to us to where we now say it to ourselves. Really, when did *you* start thinking you wouldn't succeed or that you weren't a loyal friend or an intelligent person? For better and worse, words have been a primary determinant of who we are, and our present speech will shape much of who we become.

Finally, because it is mirroring God to use our voice in shaping His kingdom here on earth, you must know that speaking sentiments from a selfish perspective does not work. It's as if selfishness nullifies the positive, life-giving effect. If someone is disingenuously speaking to another about how close he is and what good friends they are only to use them for some personal gain later, it will backfire. Usually, people can sense it. Although they might not be able to put their finger on the "what," they know there's just something keeping them feeling a little bit apprehensive or odd in the relationship. I've seen this happen when certain sales representatives attend a church to obtain the mailing list and meet friends/potential customers.

The scheme to silence

As workmanships of a creative, loving, molding, active God, we reflect the same attributes. We can create, love, and give because we're made in His image. And the way in which much of this occurs is through our voice. God gave us His Words, and we are to be rooted in them. Much of His creative, moving, loving communication occurs as we listen for His voice in any and every form. Our voice is the same, on a human scale. The idea of "voice" is the unique, shaping, creating force that comes out of us as a one-of-a-kind creation of God. Just as each person has his or her own thumbprint that can't be copied by another, so each is supposed to have a distinctive "voice." It's a larger concept than mere speaking. A synonym for voice is "influence." That's it – as children of God, our unique voice is meant to further God's work on this earth and bring Him glory. We are meant to have significant influence through our shaping, creating, loving, unique expressions. Our voice is more than just speaking; it is the idea of how all that makes us "us" comes out in expressions and manifestations unique to us. It encompasses our self, and the way our uniqueness impacts the world around. It is through communicated through our speech, our actions, our creating, our emoting, and even our silence. This expression of self is exclusive to us, so no one else can speak for us.

The fact that our unique voice is to be a building block in the construction of God's kingdom makes it a primary target for evil. The powers of hell want to silence our beautiful, God-made voice in any way possible. Wickedness will try to shut you up in any way possible. Satan and his minions also know God's truth that the tongue contains the power of life and death. They know a single statement can derail a life with tremendous potential for God, if given by the right person at the right time. The assault on our voices as the instruments of incredible power God made them for cannot be taken too lightly. Evil assaults our "speaking" because of its power. Can you think of the ways in which people's voices are attacked?

Sexual abuse survivors know this all too well. Their entire sense that they have a right to say "no" in such a way that it will be heard and respected is decimated by the abuse.

Children whose parents physically hurt them often have their voices twisted to become over-voices – too much, too big, always forceful, defensive, and overpowering. This is a distortion of the voice God intended. When people want to forcefully overpower another, what do they do? Put a hand over that person's mouth or gag him. Suffocation ultimately kills someone. These are pictures of what evil wants to do with our God-given, God-propelled, God-empowered voice as we speak. Thinking our words are unimportant, that what we say is stupid, or that we have no right to our opinion show just a few ways in which evil wins the battle of silencing us. If your voice has been silenced through some hurtful experience or person, see it for what it is and this day begin using your powerful God-made instrument once again in His service.

The scheme to silence us is comprehensive. This would not be the case if our voices, words, and speech were not so incredibly valuable. If nothing else, I want this chapter to remind us to *speak*. However, for it to be an effective tool for developing relationships, strengthening friendships, and building the body of Christ, we must use the tool in the correct way. Everyone knows how helpful a hammer is when used for the right purposes, but when not handled well, it leaves damage. It's the same with our words. We can be extremely effectual or extremely injurious with our words. Therefore, we must constantly choose them intentionally. And carefully. Even in the middle of a spat, or should I say *especially* in the middle of a spat? Even when you are just "needing to vent" (which, because of the power of speaking, I do not recommend). Even when we are just chilling with our closest buds. Proverbs gives us an apt caution about haphazard words: "When words are many, sin is not absent" (Proverbs 10:19).

How are you saying what you are saying?

Another tool to developing good relationships is found in knowing how people communicate with one another. For instance, some people communicate quite literally while others speak frequently in analogies. Some individuals can only express themselves through word pictures while others have an exacting command of the English language. There are people who exaggerate to make their feelings known and some who articulate thoughts by conveying stories. There are literal people and intuitive people. There are maximizers, or ones who enhance everything they say, and there are minimizers, ones who shrink the particular topic to be less important. God has truly made each of His creations unique and wonderful. Being able to identify even just a smidgen of how someone typically communicates can be a huge relationship builder.

Think now of your closest friends and relatives. Who speaks in analogies? Which one always uses extreme language? Who is the storyteller? How about yourself? Listening closely to how others express themselves can really open up communication to a new level. If you figure out that your closest friend articulates his deepest feelings through word pictures, you have uncovered a way to significantly enrich that relationship. You'll know when he says, "It's like there's a spider trapped in its own web" that he's probably feeling overwhelmed, ensnared in sin, or caught in some circumstances. If your mother-in-law is extremely literal, then you will benefit by listening to the exact words she says and by being sure to say precisely what you mean when the two of you are in conversation. If she says to give her a call in the next "couple of days," then you have precisely two days to do it!

Watching for how people express their emotions is very important. It's also a fascinating exercise. For instance, a person who processes internally won't express his emotions verbally, but might forward you a song or hand you a DVD. This is his emotional language! Clues to how they feel about you, the world, and themselves can be found therein. Other people will often speak in analogies. You've heard them... "I feel like a train wreck," or "The other shoe might as well drop," or "It's like being a piece of bread in a parking lot filled with pigeons." Such a person is expressing her feelings, not just providing amusing dialogue. Others will use third-person references. I've seen this happen a lot with people who spend much of life compartmentalizing or putting things in categories, like business executives. You can hear them say phrases like, "A guy could probably get really angry over something like that," or "You just never know when that's going to bother a person," or "You just wonder if things are ever going to change." Catching how another person is expressing his or her true emotion can be a hard thing to do if you're not looking for it, but once you do, it often seems blatantly obvious. When your friend "just needs to get in a good round of golf" or off-handedly mentions that she was on monster.com this past week, he or she is giving you clues to deeper feelings of insecurity, stress, or anxiety.

One type of processing that is frequently a relationship bungler is the black-or-white, all-or-none, either/or variety. Things are either healthy or unhealthy, wonderful or awful, stupid or smart, ugly or pretty, etc. Many people think this way, and unfortunately, many of those who do process in the all-or-none fashion are emotionally young. I just had a conversation with my son who said that when I reprimand him, it feels like that "other stuff I say about him being great" isn't true. He's a child and his brain has quite literally not developed the capacity for abstract thought yet. So, he either feels like a "bad kid" or a "good kid," rather than the reality – which is he is a great kid who sometimes does bad things. A client of mine also spoke yesterday about her propensity to think this way and how it sabotages her newfound relationship. (God certainly knew I would be writing about this today!) She quickly sways from "we have a great relationship because there are no problems right now" to "we are having a problem, so that means our relationship is bad and must be ended." Can you see how processing things in this way is quite out of touch with the reality that nothing is ever *completely* one way or another? Her relationship is a growing one which will have some good and bad aspects intermingled – *that's what a relationship is!* No human, therefore no human interaction, will ever be 100% great. Perfection in relationships does not exist.

To perceive things in this categorical way is severely delimiting. Again, so very many people think this way without realizing it. Is this you? It reminds me of Old Testament law. The clear, stringent rules and regulations could not be kept by anyone. This is why Jesus came, and in His coming, He fulfilled and abolished the law. Now we live in the Spirit and are judged not by behavior, but by motivations, not by a checklist, but by the heart (Ephesians 2:15, Matthew 5). A black or white framework for life sets someone up to struggle with the sin of being judgmental. In their eyes, people are either sinners or saved, godly or ungodly. Isn't the truth for all of us who have accepted Christ that we are now godly, becoming so more and more every day by God's work of sanctification, but still struggle with sin regularly? It's Paul's depiction in

Romans 7 – we sin in ways that we hate, but we ourselves are fully righteous because of Christ.

At the risk of belaboring the point, black or white styles of relating, and especially of communicating, shut relationships down. Others might feel, as a friend, that they are given few options for interaction. Think about how a spouse might be suffocated through such a stringent scheme. If the husband says he's a little angry, he might later hear his wife telling another what rage he has! (She exaggerates because of viewing everything in extremes.) If the wife asks for a little more attention when he comes from work at night, the "either/or" male might interpret her request as having to dote over her endlessly. (He swings from neglect to absorption.) Intentionally studying your closest companions' ways of perceiving and communicating can completely change your interactions.

Language that's loving

The theory of love languages speaks about how people communicate love to one another. Under the assumption that each person feels love differently, Gary Chapman has posited that there are five primary modalities by which people experience love. They are (1) physical affection, (2) acts of service, (3) words of affirmation, (4) gifts, and (5) quality time.[56] Whatever love language a person generally prefers for receiving love becomes the main way he or she expresses love, too. So, if a person's foremost way to experience love is through acts of service, he will generally do acts of service for other people about whom he cares. If someone feels loved most by words of affirmation, she will be very encouraging to others whom she loves. For the "gifts" love language person, picking out a present can take an exorbitant amount of time. If someone in your family has the love language of gifts, you would do well to work hard at picking a thoughtful birthday present!

My point in bringing this topic to the fore is that if we are to deepen our relationships with others, speaking another person's language is imperative. If your best friend only spoke German, sooner or later you would learn some of the German language. If you were really committed to this friend, you would intentionally take lessons to communicate in his or her language. It's the same with speaking "love" to each other. If your spouse feels most loved by quality time, you can *do* all you want for her in acts of service, but it won't have the impact you desire. She just wants to spend time with you, and that will strengthen your bond because you have spoken in her language. Similarly, if someone experiences love through words of affirmation, giving him all the gifts in the world will never bring you as close as an encouraging note, a word of appreciation, or a card expressing what he means to you.

Mike and I have had to learn new languages. He gets filled up and feels closeness through the way his family was growing up – spending quality time together. Just hanging out watching a football game or something similar feels comfortable and good. My love language is words of affirmation. The more, the better! There's no such thing as too much encouragement. So, obviously, when I want to let Mike know how much I love him, I tell him – going on about how great he is, what an amazing man, leader, and father he is, and how I wouldn't want anyone else but him. Imagine how mind-numbing it was for me in our early years when I could literally see those precious words I was giving bounce off him and land on the floor!! To my shock and dismay, they weren't going in. Words of affirmation don't go in very deeply for him. So, I realized after many years that if I really want to show Mike that I enjoy who he is, I just sit quietly down beside him in front of the football game!!

This brings up a final point about how we get our love languages. From counseling throughout the years, I've observed that people generally feel love either by how they *did* get love in their growing up years, or how they *didn't*. Some people who grew up wealthy are deeply loved by receiving a gift. Others who grew up in a family that showed physical affection are very touchy, enjoying all types of physical connection from a simple hug to sexual contact. The opposite is also true, however. The person who was never told "I love you," can quite literally never have enough words of affirmation. People who grew up poor can feel most loved through a gift. Some people literally crave a hug because of how few they've received in life.

What is your love language? Have you ever thought about why? Maybe you are overwhelmed by acts of service people do for you because you had to be so responsible at such a young age. Perhaps you feel very connected to people who spend time with you because your sickly sibling necessarily consumed all of your parents' time and attention. Gifts could "do it" for you because of how careful your grandma was to select the perfect gift, wrapped with great care, and given with surrounding fanfare. Whatever it is, it's important for you to learn how to recognize when other people are showing you love in *their* languages, too.

As well, if you are serious about deepening your soul connections with certain people in your life, teaching yourself how to speak their languages will give you great mileage down the relational road. I have one friend who I love and appreciate, but whose love language is not words of affirmation. Instead of verbally praising her, I find a way to spend time with her. And, she tries to love me through what feels like awkward verbal utterances! My other soul friend is ultra touched by gifts. This is practically a foreign language to me, so I have to elicit help in learning it.

The bottom line is that people are worth it. Living out God's command to give, bless, encourage, and lift others up always brings a peaceful "yes" inside from His Holy Spirit. God will give you the ability to actually "hear" another person's processing, emotional language, or love language. What it requires is the desire – the ability will follow when the desire is present. Watching your language and paying close attention to others' captures an unlimited tool for relational development.

Chapter Nine
LIMIT YOUR EXPECTATIONS

Inappropriate expectations can kill any good relationship. People have broken off contact over unreturned phone calls, delinquent thank-you notes, and closed invitation lists. Spouses have divorced over the loss of romance or disappearance of passion. Friends have parted after discovering another's past, seeing the way another's home is kept, or listening to how someone speaks to his or her children. Really, where do our expectations come from? Were we to ask if you thought there was any one perfect person, you would surely disagree. But, this is how we often unconsciously think in relationships. While there is not one human who doesn't fail at some point, it is infinitely hard not to have standards for others in our lives. Perhaps this is why we often treat the people who are the closest to us the worst. We have a very high bar for them because we depend on them to meet our needs, and if they don't, it's painful. Whatever the case, expectations under control is what makes for true soul connection.

Is this elevator going up?

Why is it so challenging for us to stay grounded in the reality that every human being puts his or her pants on one leg at a time? Instead, when we see people who seem to have things a bit more together than how we assess ourselves, we begin elevating them. It starts innocently enough – admiring others' giftedness, skills, accomplishments or qualities. We imagine that they don't struggle with the things we do, and sometimes begin putting them on a pedestal in our minds. It's good and right that the people we think highly of provide us examples for how to do certain things and be certain ways. All too subtly, though, elevating people slips into a problem. That problem is unrealistic expectations. We transfer thoughts about how excellent they are in some ways to mean they are excellent in all ways. When we elevate others above where they should be, there is only one place for them to go – down.

When we regard others too highly, we then become disappointed when they fail to meet the arbitrary expectations we have assigned. To expect the pastor who is fantastic at preaching to also lead meetings well could be fallacious. Imagining that your exceptional boss is a wonderful mother might be erroneous. To suppose that your fantastic Christian professor would never struggle with lust could be mistaken. The danger in idyllic perspectives is that when we catch glimpses that others are failing our expectations, we can then turn critical, angry, and even bitter. Oftentimes bitterness comes when we have expectations, and they are not met. Of bitterness, an excellent quote I heard is that "bitterness remembers details."[57] I imagine it would be true that if you have people under the microscope of high expectations, assessing them by the minutia of their lives could lead to remembering details.

A few years back, there was a young woman who approached me after a conference at which I spoke. She happened to live in the same city as I and had just begun attending the same large church. Therefore, she asked if I could mentor her, and if she could spend time hanging out with my family. In a challenging conversation, I shared with her that the level to which I would be able to interact with her would be less than she desired. Based upon some things she said, I also told her that I would end up disappointing her now or disappointing her later. I could disappoint her now by not being as accessible as she had hoped or disappoint her later when she realized I am a person who is far from perfect. In other words, her expectations of who I was and what I could do were clearly too high. She now thanks me for that initially rough conversation because it helped her have appropriate expectations of me (but she admits she was still disappointed).

How do you handle others' imperfections? Do you accept them, laugh at them, become hurt by them, or resent them? What expectations of your family members do you have that could be too high? In what ways are your expectations too low? (This is rarely a problem. Normally we anticipate too much.) To be human *is* to be inconsistent. Therefore, the true assessment of a person is to look at his or her character over time. If we are waiting for someone we are in relationship with to be completely consistent – responding well every time, predictable in his or her emotional patterns, unaffected by hormones and sleep – then we will wait a long time.

And for Christians, do we understand that there is no such thing as "advanced Christianity"? Every person who begins his or her Christian life begins it with all he or she needs. There's not "more" or "less" of Jesus. Yes, there's sanctification and learning to die to self and cultivating hearing the voice of God and maturing. However, the Christian life is not some outcome that a person works hard to achieve. Do not be confused by a good works mentality, which leads to law, which leads to death (Galatians 3:10-14, Romans 7:10,

Romans 8:2). The Christian life is the life of Christ in a believer. Christ is more obviously manifest as a believer becomes more surrendered, humble, and yielding. The Christian life is not something we do, it is something *Christ* does in us through the presence of His Spirit. (Romans 7:6, 8:2-4; Galatians 3:2-5, 3:14; Philippians 3:3). With that said, what is wrong with this type of perspective: "I heard that person curse the other day, so he must not be as spiritual as I thought"? Do you think, "I can't believe it!" when a Christian leader or close Christian friend falls? Such a reaction reveals the expectation that a Christian who has shown marks of maturity won't sin. For the sake of making Jesus bigger and humans smaller, I pray we rid ourselves of such expectations.

Good 'n healthy

The question then becomes twofold: What are healthy and appropriate expectations, and how do we recognize when they are too high? In this section, we'll look at a few cues for how to manage this tough relational area. Generally speaking, instead of looking for perfect people, we can be grateful for the flawed, ordinary ones God has given us. We can cease being *Laugh at yourself!* disappointed by refusing to put people on pedestals in the first place. We can stop criticizing people in our lives for their imperfections and start accepting them as they are. Mostly, when it comes to the area of expectations, we can first look in the mirror and then look to the Lord. When we examine ourselves, we can squarely observe our own flaws and hopefully laugh at ourselves. (This is a sign of true maturity.) When we look to the Lord, we realize He really is the only One who will never desert, forsake, fail, be inconsistent, abandon, or

153

betray us (Hebrews 13:5; Deuteronomy 4:31, 7:9; Psalm 89:33, 37:28).

I play a great deal of competitive tennis, and there is something about this sport and most others that is maddening. It is this – you are only as good as your last success or failure. In other words, people have very short memories. For our relationships to be lasting and true, we have to develop a longer-term perspective. You can't evaluate your friend on the one errant word she said in a tired mess last week while you forget the faithful presence she's been in your life to date. So, to combat the danger of expectations, force yourself to take a more wide-angle-lens view of a relationship. If someone erupts and spews some ugliness, but has never before done that in your five-year friendship, take your history in context when assimilating the content of the unusual eruption. The implementation here is to remember who someone has shown herself to be *over time.*

Another tool for adjusting your expectations concerns those people from whom you would expect love and encouragement, but who do not routinely offer it. Some adults to this day become upset when they look to a parent for support and instead receive something else. Though the grown child can know the parent is not likely to change in this regard, every time he or she gets off the phone or reads an email, disappointment occurs all over again. Why? The answer is found in expectations. This son or daughter has never adjusted expectations of his or her parent. Maybe it's because they look around and see other parents providing much wonderful support, even of grown children and, especially, of grandchildren. Maybe it's because they have some infantile hope that something will make the parent change. Although it is cause for sadness and grief, the adult child must at some point adjust expectations to match reality if he or she is going to mature. If not, the result will be a stuck, confused, hopeless, and perhaps bitter person.

What I recommend is to envision a surprise UPS package that shows up on your doorstep. You weren't expecting it, but it is filled with your favorite things – just what you needed and wanted. You unwrap it with great delight and savor all the treats within, taking the time to adequately go through it and enjoy it completely. However, you don't expect that a package will show up on your doorstep tomorrow or the next day or ever again. You simply are grateful for what you got. You don't spend your entire life and energy staring out the window wondering how to get another package like that. This is how to best view the times when we are supported, loved well, encouraged, affirmed, cared for, or made to feel valuable by people who don't normally make us feel that way. When it comes, enjoy it totally, to the max. Thankfully drink in all the good feelings and thoughts that come along with it, but do not expect that it will happen again. If your rich grandmother has never given you any money even though you've seen her give it to others, don't think that because she sent you one check, she's going to suddenly change a lifetime pattern. If your dad just wasn't "big on words" and he tells you he's proud of you in a rare moment, don't be surprised if that's all you get. Enjoy it for what it is. Adjusting our expectations to what is actual rather than what is hoped for is ultimately a healthier posture for us, even though it may carry some grief and pain along with those unmet needs and desires.

Expectation-wise, when it comes to precious UPS packages full of what we want and need from other people, it is best not to anticipate receiving from others what they don't give. If we think of it as the unexpected, yet wonderful, surprise that shows up, that is good. However, if we want something from someone who has never given it before, we must ask ourselves why we are looking for it from this person. If we don't know what we're doing, we'll keep looking to others over and over again with the same results. Such has been described as the definition of insanity. We also sabotage ourselves when we're constantly looking to everyone else's doorsteps to see what "UPS packages" they are getting. If we obsess about what must be inside others' "packages" from their friends and loved ones, we will never have a chance to better our own relationships. A client of mine with whom I was using this analogy said sadly, "I think I'm going around trying to steal everyone else's packages from their porches." She never had a mother or father to speak of and realized how this interfered with relational expectations of every kind in her life.

It's good to apply this to other people, too. Lowering or adjusting your expectations of someone to match his or her capabilities, maturity, personality, and experiences helps us have better relationships. Soul connections happen more naturally when we understand and operate within the sphere that all people have some strengths and some weaknesses. At some point in every relationship, those weaknesses are going to bother or hurt us. Discerning what is healthy or unhealthy - in terms of what we desire from others - will help us better handle the weaknesses of others.

One avenue to wisdom in this area is to ask others what their ideas of appropriate expectations are and what they are not. For example, is it okay to expect a spouse to be in a good mood every day? No. For him or her to treat you respectfully no matter what his or her mood? Yes. For your marital relationship to be filled with the same passion you had when dating? No. For you to need your spouse to show you attention and love in ways that connect with your soul? Yes. For your friend to call you every day? No. For a good friend to have a general idea about your life and stay connected concerning the big things going on with you? Yes. For your close friend to not have other close friends or to include you in everything he or she is doing? No. For a buddy to initiate with you on a regular basis? Yes, if he or she is an initiator in general, but no, if he or she doesn't ever initiate with anyone. For your pastor to come to the hospital when you are having gall bladder surgery? No. For your pastor to come to the hospital when your child has been in a serious accident? Yes. For your pastor to come to the hospital at all when his church is 3,000 members? No.

Generally, it does work to treat others as you would want to be treated. (God's principles really do work!!) (Matthew 7:12, 23:29) You wouldn't want people to expect you to call every day or always be in a good mood or buy them extravagant gifts on holidays. However, we also need to be sure we are giving room for those love language and communication differences talked about in the previous chapter. We may actually have a close ally who is reaching out to us, but we are not "catching it" because of our expectations. This reminds me of what happened when the people in Bible times were longing for a Savior. They were eagerly desirous of One who would come and redeem the world and anticipated His arrival with hope. What happened, though? Because of their inappropriate expectations, they missed Him altogether (John 10:24-39 is one example). Their minds were so focused on what they wanted and thought a Savior would be that they missed Jesus. Are we so intent on what a high-quality friend/

spouse/boss/mother (you fill in the blank) is that we miss out on the good one we have right in front of our faces? Recall the concept from chapter six to focus on what *is* instead of what is not. When we have that vantage point, our expectations lose their stranglehold.

Inny versus outy

A particularly helpful aspect of adjusting our expectations is being able to differentiate when someone is an internal processor or an external processor. Especially in close relationships, like marriage, possessing this knowledge prevents many hurt feelings and improves relational happiness. When someone is an internal processor, it means that things become clear to him or her *inside* him or herself. An internal processor takes in information while in the context of other people, but gains insight and understanding of it internally, usually alone. Clarity comes within a person, not external to him or her. Things must make sense inside. This person will listen, take notes, and absorb data, but assimilation of that data into prior knowledge, larger frameworks, and daily functioning does not occur until he or she has had time to stew on it. Internal processors *must* have time to allow information to marinate. Like coffee, new input must be percolated before it is ready for consumption. This is why internal processors can often seem slow or even resistant when encountering new information.

Relating to internal processors can be challenging if you don't realize who you're dealing with. The typical pattern is that they will listen to you and look at you and even be intent on what you are saying…to a point. Then, they're done. Full. And the gauge that indicates said fullness to the rest of us is *that look*. Their eyes glaze over, and they pretty much stop interacting. All hope of continued conversation is lost. Now, if we do not understand what is happening and continue to try to elicit words from them, we become increasingly frustrated with their minimal responses. We are hurt by these people if we lack insight into what is really going on.

Remember, things become clear *inside* of internal processors, not in the exchange between humans. To personalize when they are "done" in conversation is a common mistake people make. When their eyes glaze over, if we can realize that they simply can't take any more information in, we do much better than if we draw conclusions about their regard for us. It's not that they don't want to engage with us; it's that they have no more room in the "in" box. It's not personal. He or she isn't trying to hurt your feelings. (I can hear the internal processors shouting "Amen!" even now!)

Newly acquired information needs to be steeped like a tea bag for internal processors. This is why they dream regularly. Most internal processors dream almost nightly and remember them well. They often consume movies and find layers of expressive meaning through music. Painters will produce their best work as their strong emotion comes out through their fingertips. Their clarity on matters comes very rarely through language, but via more intangible, non-verbal ways. Because of this, they often need time and space that others can find troubling, if they lack understanding. Time and space are the only ingredients that permit the internal processor to eventually reengage.

External processors, on the other hand get clarity on matters in the space *outside* of themselves. They thrive on dialogue and interchange wherein information is collected, sifted, and new insights are formed. External processors are often talkers, and can be heard saying things like, "I never realized such-and-so until it was just coming out of my mouth" or "I never knew I felt that way before we were just talking about it." Realizations come to them in discussions with others, journaling, emails, workbooks and the like. The key difference is that the processing space is outside of their being. In meetings, these are the people that thrive, barely being able to refrain from peppering multiple ideas off others. The extreme external processor can seem relentless, and might sometimes be avoided by those who don't have time for a long conversation or the energy for a lively dialogue.

External processors thrive on being drawn out, feel loved by being listened to, and are enthralled with conversation. As a result of their excitement, they can speak over others. They can also fail to choose their words carefully, as processing the idea is more important than the particulars of an issue. Just as external processors should know not to be hurt by the internal processor's need for space to sift, the internal processor cannot personalize the external processor's seemingly carelessness in conversation.

While I've just painted a picture of two ends of a continuum, most everyone generally falls in one of the categories. Are you an internal processor, who wonders why you can't quite "hang" in conversations like others? Do you have enough nightly dreams to warrant a log to actually track them? Do you find your thoughts are muddled until you can sit on the porch with your coffee? Or are you the external processor, whose thoughts can make you feel stuck until you can converse about them? Do you need to process your feelings in a journal before you can sleep at night? Understanding who you are is very helpful and important. Understanding which of these types others in your lives are can radically alter your relationships.

For instance, I used to routinely get hurt that my husband seemed to have such little tolerance for listening to me. If he didn't quickly force me to the "bottom line" in a conversation, he would zone out before long. He would then vehemently deny my subsequent accusation that he just didn't care enough about me. Suffice it to say that after taking personality tests and following Covey's guiding principle (seek to understand)[58], we now have much more harmonious dialogue. Without an understanding of what was really happening, I took it personally and was offended.

It's true that internal and external processors are often stereotyped down gender lines. Males are portrayed as internal processors; women external. In his work on marital couples, John Gray has shown that men do indeed have a need for cave time, or a pattern of retreat wherein they get recharged.[59] While these are helpful, it's not always the case that women are the incessant talkers and men the strong, silent types. I've actually found in all my years of counseling others that each couple typically has one more "male," logical, factual, non-emotional person and one more "female," sensitive, intuitive, relational person. It is surprising how often these do *not* follow gender lines. It's the same for internal and external processors. Each couple typically has one of each type.

The important takeaway for all of us on this point is that every relationship will improve if we understand inherent personality differences. Secondarily, there are things we can do with knowledge of who we personally are which will reap great benefit. For the external processor, it's imperative that you not personalize when the internal processor with whom you are relating is "full." You can promote unity and closeness by being more concise, giving him or her a road map of where you are going, and especially by giving the bottom line first. While that might be hard for an external processor to swallow, if you give an internal processor the bottom line first, he or she will actually be more able to engage with you in dialogue. Setting expectations up front is also extremely effective. Saying "I just need you to listen," or "I really need help with this issue," sets your conversation up for success. Your best gift to internal processors is following an engagement/release pattern. If they know there is a beginning and end to this processing time, they can hang in there much easier than an open-ended, ongoing dialogue.

If you are an internal processor, there's one primary gift you can give your external processing friends. *Let them know you are reaching your capacity, and commit to getting back with them.* In other words, if you will promise to circle back around with further thoughts in a day or so, then you are blessing your friend. This is the most common error internal processors make – not letting others know what's going on inside. By definition, they really can't express such a sentiment well. Therefore, I advocate having a hip-pocket phrase because it can really help matters. Here's an example: "Hey, I'm enjoying this conversation, but am reaching my max. I'll be sure we pick this up again tomorrow." Apply it to a recent conversation you've had – yes, even with your spouse – and imagine the difference. It sends the external processor the message that you care while still representing accurately your state of mind.

In summary, when we have a clearer picture of how a person thinks, what someone does and does not have to offer, and what we ourselves are hoping for, we increase our odds of having a good relationship. When we are not aware of the expectations we are bringing to the table, we can often experience across-the-board disappointment with others and wonder why. Limiting our expectations to what is appropriate and actually attainable will definitely help clear the way to true soul connection. Concerning our relationships, it's crucial to remember we are more blessed when we are more forgiving, when we are more willing to love people as they are rather than as we want them to be, and when we are looking through the lens of Jesus' grace. When that is our viewpoint, disappointed expectations are not in the picture.

LOOK IN THE MIRROR
Chapter Ten

Who doesn't love a good, long look in the mirror? Pretty much no one! Well, for true connection between souls to occur, it requires a figurative look in the mirror. And the one we are talking about is not the mirror in the small mauve bathroom or the one in your bedroom illuminated by your night light. No, we're talking about the mirror in your car in the broad daylight, the one at the beauty shop under the fluorescent lights, or the glaring one in the dressing room when you are trying on bathing suits. Think about the difference in these views. I look fantastic in my downstairs bathroom and disgusting in my upstairs bathroom. Why? It's because of the brightness and fullness of the surrounding light. For our relationships to be substantive and enriching, we must first take a long, hard look in the mirror of our own strengths, weaknesses, patterns, and motives before we move anywhere else.

To submit ourselves to such inspection is biblical. The Psalmist records, "Search me, O God, and know my heart. Try me and know my anxious thoughts, see if there be any offensive way in me and lead me in the way everlasting" (Psalm 139:23-24). As well, "All my longings lie open before you" (Psalm 38:9). When we are willing to look in the mirror of our own selves – expectations, shortcomings, idiosyncrasies, relational rules, petty disturbances, and unforgiveness – only then can truly reciprocal relationships happen. Otherwise, we don't realize our own blind spots cause problems to others just as theirs do to us. It's the picture that Jesus spoke of when He said we were focused on others' specks, as we peer around our own logs (Matthew 7:3).

If we don't look within, at just the moment we need to see ourselves, we are often preoccupied with another's way of treating us. We sit in judgment of a friend who has hurt us by betraying a confidence, not remembering that in God's system, our judgment is just as bad as his or her betrayal. It is hard to be concerned about a slight edge in our tone of voice toward someone who has spread gossip about us. Our cool aloofness can be just as damaging to a spouse as his or her temper is to us. However, without knowing it, we determine arbitrary levels of what is more and less acceptable, and then sit smugly in the victim seat.

Although perhaps overstating it here, there is truth for all of us to heed. Pharisaical-like attitudes are ready to sneak in at every turn. We are all sinners in desperate need of God's grace. There is no one righteous, not even one (Romans 3:9). To humble ourselves in gratitude for a God who has rescued us will help our relationships immensely. Instead of being upset about how others are not meeting our needs or loving us well enough, we'll find ourselves just grateful that others will be in any type of relationship with our pitiful selves at all! Whenever I start to think I am "all that," I'm so thankful the Lord reminds me I'm just incredibly blessed by friends and family who put up with me – ever! It's like we forget that we aggravate and hurt others as much as they do us.

Clean your cup, water your grass

It is true that we need to allow God to search us and right our perspective on ourselves so that we enter into relationships with humility. This is what a proverbial look in the mirror of our own souls will help us to do. Take inventory now – what irritates you? What type of personality do you find challenging to be around? What about you is hard for others to be around? Do you yourself have a preference that becomes a demand for others around you (how the dishes are placed in the dishwasher, within how much time a phone call should be returned, who should pay for dinner)? What do you expect of others that you personally fail in?

Looking in the mirror and allowing our own flaws to be in full view is critical if we want true friendships. Really, such a stance can transform our entire relationships. Jenn testified of this to me last week. She had contacted me months ago about getting in to see me for counseling, saying that she was "at the end of her rope" with her husband and the state of her marriage. We were not able to connect and begin counseling. In response to a follow-up email I sent, she replied no longer needing help. She told me that a health crisis had occurred in her family which completely changed her focus. She said, "I have been so blessed to have my eyes opened to a world so much bigger than me and my personal issues, my focus has completely changed. When I originally emailed you, I was at a turning point in my marriage and desperately wanted to throw in the towel. I didn't, and now God has made our marriage stronger than it has been in our eight years together. I am excited to see what opportunities God gives us next!" This amazing shift happened because her focus was forced to shift in the family crisis. Every time we take our eyes off our own demands, feelings, and sense of justice, discontentment drifts away. It's true.

The saying, "The grass is always greener on the other side" is well-known. It speaks of the rampant human tendency toward envy. Awhile back, I heard a great twist on it. "If the grass is greener on the other side, you may want to try watering your own grass." What a fantastic admonition for us. We need to take our eyes off everyone else and what they are doing and put some effort into working on our own stuff. When we water our personal "grass" by looking at *our* own impatience, *our* quick judgmentalism, or the way *we* hold grudges, then our relationships with others will have a real chance to improve. Watering your own turf in marriages, in friendships, with children, and with extended family can bear fruit you can't see today, but will see in the future. If we put forth effort, prayer, and humility towards how we can better love others, then our relationships will improve, guaranteed. Paul told us being like Jesus should be our aim: "Do nothing out of selfish ambition or vain conceit, but in humility consider others better than yourselves. Each of you should look not only to your own interests, but also to the interests of others" (Philippians 2:3-4). Selfishly wanting others to change, thinking we are above others, and desiring others to be more attuned to our needs are all things a true look at ourselves can uncover.

Whenever we have our eyes somewhere other than on our own shortcomings, we are in danger of committing the same sin as the Pharisees. "You blind Pharisee, first clean the inside of the cup and of the dish, so that the outside of it may become clean also" (Matthew 23:26). Jesus confronted the fact that outwardly they appeared righteous, but inwardly were filled with hypocrisy and a lack of self-control. Do you look good to everyone else, but have ugly thoughts about others reigning internally? Taking a figurative look in the mirror of our own hearts might just be the single most important piece of advice gleaned from reading this book.

Our propensity for having double standards is nauseatingly prevalent. We want others to be consistent, and we are not. We expect others to be unselfish, and we are selfish in wanting them to act unselfishly. We desire our friends to never think ill of us, and yet we do them. I belong to a goal-oriented group that has a variety of people in it. In my time with them, I have observed a pattern that the favorite pastime seems to be talking about others. I was telling someone recently about how tough it is to be in that environment because I know the minute I get up and leave, I will be gossiped about. While my friend did what I wanted, which was empathizing with my plight, the Holy Spirit did not. I was in effect gossiping to another about how this group of women gossips. While I did not name names, I was guilty of having a double standard. It was not okay for them to talk about me, but it was okay for me to talk about them (because of some flimsy excuse like not naming names). I feel Paul's sentiment when he said, "Oh, wretched man that I am!" (Romans 7:28). We are innocent of having double standards only when our eyes are squarely on our own sin.

We all too often interpret others' actions by our standards. This causes us to put words in each others' mouths and attribute motives and thoughts to them that they in actuality are not thinking! A simple example is the wife who asks the husband if he likes what she has chosen to wear. He says he does, but she abruptly runs to change the outfit. Why? Because he didn't say it "like he meant it" or it was "in a weird tone" and instead of taking him at his word, she put words in his mouth. We so very often respond to what we decide another person was thinking, rather than believing what he or she was saying. We assume without asking. We judge based upon what actions we can see, what facial expressions we observe, and how others respond to our conversation. This points us back to a principle given in chapter two: When in doubt, check it out. If you have purposed to believe the best in a relationship, but still think you sense another's unsettled attitude, ask him if your assumptions have any validity. Generally, if we are instead focused on how we can improve a relationship by being kinder, more forgiving, gracious, patient, long-suffering, understanding, empathic – any such movement! – the outcome will be a closer connection with the ones we love.

The relational mirror

The loud point being made here is that we must be looking in the mirror of our own flawed nature to have true soul connecting relationships. However, there is another mirroring reference here that can also be helpful. It is that our relationships themselves reflect back to us truths about ourselves. In other words, if you are having a tough time evaluating your own strengths and weaknesses as you think about the relationships you have, look at your connections with others across the board. They will tell you a great deal!

If every relationship you have involves people who disappoint you, you probably have too high or misplaced expectations. If in general people don't really get back to you after you initiate with them, it might be because you are unknowingly demanding. Do you observe that some people avoid you? Perhaps they find you critical or overly talkative.

Is there drama at every turn in your life? Then you are doing something to create or add to it. Does it seem like others use you as a dumping ground for all their internal grumblings? They might be mirroring to you that you are a good listener, a compassionate person, or conversely, a commiserator. Do others call you when they are down? You're probably an encourager, or grounded in God's Word. Whether a positive reflection or a negative one, if we step back and look at our relationships across the board, they definitely speak to us about who we are and what it's like to be around us. If you have the maturity to straightforwardly ask your friends and loved ones, "What's it like to be around me?", their answers will undoubtedly be enlightening.

Kay Arthur agrees and says that our dealings with others indicate our spiritual state. She offers that "a righteous walk with God will always manifest in our relationships with our fellow man. The two are inseparable, for our righteousness is demonstrated in our treatment of one another."[60] We are called to walk as Jesus did. He taught, "In everything, therefore, treat people the same way you want them to treat you, for this is the Law and the Prophets" (Matthew 7:12). This "golden rule" is telling us to give away the unconditional love that we so desperately want ourselves. Commit yourself to the highest good of others, and *that* will be following Jesus' relational footsteps. Can you imagine what a difference it would make in our world if every one of God's children lived this way? Instead, though, we "generally have great patience and tolerance for our own shortcomings, and are quite impatient with others' rates of change."[61] Allow a probing look at how you interact with others to reveal to you whether you live by the golden rule or your own set of rules.

Crack in the mirror

The other revelation a look in the mirror of our relationships will give is how deeply our wounds have impacted our
lives. Every hurt we have shows up in our relationships. We
can keep them under wraps at work, but we can't hide them
when we're with family and friends. If someone important
betrayed you, you'll probably struggle with trust. Distrust of
others is one of the most common results of emotional hurt.
I still have a hard time believing Mike after all these years.
While I honestly don't think there's a more trustworthy person
on the face of the planet, I have to force myself to believe
him when he speaks love to me. It's much less so than when
we were first married, but I still occasionally question his
motives. How tiring that must be to have to live with! What is
the result of your wounds that keeps showing itself through
your relationships? A pervasive sense of shame when others
get to know you? A protective tendency to pull away when
someone else comes close?

Just tonight I talked with someone who was abandoned when she was five, and remembers her mother walking
off without her in a grocery store. She can vividly recall that
horrifying feeling, so she doesn't allow people to really know
her for fear that if they see her true neediness, they will leave,
too. How frustrating for others who sincerely enjoy her to
feel her keep them at arm's length. From her vantage point, it
doesn't seem like anyone really wants to know her. She can't
see how she contributes to the series of events that leaves her
feeling abandoned by others. We all have patterns like this
that we can see if we take a broad-scope survey of our primary
relationships.

Looking in the mirror will enable us to observe where
we are weak, but also where God has strengthened, blessed,

and equipped us. While forgiveness might be excruciating for someone else, it might come rather easily for you. Perhaps you are able to empathize with others or give godly counsel or identify needs when people are in crises. Bless the Lord for the ways in which you are strong relationally and be sure to work hard to exercise these gifts. If you are great at drawing others out, volunteer to facilitate a small group at church. If hospitality comes easy, open your home. If you know how to turn a conversation – please use this when others are beginning to gossip or someone seems open to the gospel! Whatever your gifts and your wounds, intimate knowledge of them both can drastically improve your relationships. Seeing how we contribute to the success and failure of our relationships is an excellent place to begin having better ones!

A beautiful reflection

It is a mark of maturity to allow the Spirit of God to reveal our faults, flaws, and failings to us. Is there an area of selfishness or sin God is showing you about your relationships? If we allow the Lord to search our hearts, He'll do it in love. His character means His every interaction with us will be a loving one. He simply wants a clean temple because He knows what is best for us (1 Corinthians 3:16; 6:19, 20). Will we say, along with the Psalmist, "Examine me, O Lord, and try me; test my mind and my heart" (Psalm 26:2)? This type of openness to the Spirit's searching is a contrite heart, which pleases God. "The sacrifices of God are a broken spirit; a broken and contrite heart, O God, you will not despise" (Psalm 51:17). Jesus gave us the example of washing the disciples' feet and then said, "I gave you an example that you also should do as I did to you" (John 13:15). He would give them yet an even greater example when He laid down His life for them. This is our ultimate pathway to true soul connection. A look in the mirror gives us great perspective from which to contritely perceive ourselves. God honors those who humble themselves. He blesses the meek. His is the way of honest discernment and denial of selfish wishes.

Chapter Eleven
LEVEL YOUR FOCUS ON CHRIST

We are all searching for significance. While this is no surprise, it is important in that this truism impacts how we relate with each other. The need to believe we are significant is the driving element within the human spirit. Everyone wonders on some level if he or she matters to others. "Will I be valued for who I am?" is a query which rumbles inside us all. Since the fall, man has often failed to turn to God for the truth about himself, and instead looked to others for answers to questions of significance and value. This fact complicates many relationships.

While it is true that God has given us one another for love, support, encouragement, and true soul connection, issues of identity, purpose, and meaning can be answered by Him alone. The key word in this chapter's title "Level your focus on Christ" is "focus." In other words, when our focus becomes other people above God, then everything is out of order. People try to live life in the right order by ascribing to mottos like "J-O-Y," meaning Jesus first, others second, self third. But more often, we get lured into all manner of idolizing, fearing, or focusing on others. As we talked about in chapter two, whenever we forget that we are to look to God alone and instead turn our search for meaning onto others, not only is it unfulfilling, it backfires in the process.

Vertical or horizontal?

All too often, when we look horizontally instead of vertically for the important issues of significance, we begin to base our self-worth on what we believe others think about us. Over time, their approval matters more and more. Our hunger to be loved causes us to seek out friends, which is not inherently bad. However, when we put all our eggs in the basket of others' affirmation, we set up a dangerous cycle. Our desire for acceptance and love pressures us to perform for the praise of others. We do whatever we think we need to in order to get their love. When we get the validation we were working for, it doesn't take long before we realize we not only have to keep up that level of performance, but to get more approval, we have to do even better! When we look to humans for our inescapable need for self-worth, we begin to base who we are on what others say we are. Before we know it, we find our value completely in the fickle opinions of others.

The person who lives seeking the love and attention of others is never content. Despite all our efforts, we can never find lasting, gratifying peace if we feel we have to continually prove our worth. That's what happens when we live for other's approval – we have no peace. It's a travesty that we look to others who have a perspective as limited and darkened as our own to discover our significance! Rather than relying on God's constant, uplifting reassurance of who we are, we turn to others who judge our value by our ability to meet their standards. We spend so much time building relationships, striving to please people and win their respect. But then, after all of our sincere, conscientious effort, it takes just one unappreciative word from someone to ruin our sense of self-worth. How quickly an insensitive word can destroy the assurance we've worked so hard to achieve!

Becoming caught in this cycle is how we end up addicted to the approval of others. Our desire for acceptance pressures us to perform for the praise of others. We strive for success, pushing ourselves harder and farther, hoping that because of our effort and sacrifice, others will appreciate us more. But the person who lives only for the love and attention of others is never satisfied – at least, not for long. Despite our efforts, we will never find lasting peace if we have to continually prove ourselves to others. So, the burning question for you to consider is, "Whose opinion matters more to you than God's"? Whose approval do you want above all others? Living like this is codependency defined – "If others are happy with me, I am happy with me. If others are not, I am not." Instead, as believers, our value must be defined by the One who made us and sustains our very next breath. Galatians 1:10 asks it well, "Am I now trying to win the approval of men, or of God?"

Attempting to receive fundamental approval from others sabotages true relationship in a few ways. First, if we alter our behavior, personality, or true thoughts so someone might like us better, the person he or she approves of is not truly us. If I act like I'm outgoing simply so a certain group will accept me, when they do accept the "outgoing me," I haven't really been accepted for *me* at all! We can rightly conclude that when we get others to respond to us for a certain way we are performing, capitulating, or behaving, they don't really love us as individuals for who we are. They love us for what we are doing to make them happy. So, when we modify ourselves and strive to receive affirmation in large doses from certain people, when they do give it, it does not satisfy. Why? Because the person they accept is not actually you, but a doctored-up version of you made specifically for them. We defeat the very thing we set out to achieve by our own willingness to manipulatively amend ourselves to get what we think we want from other people.

There is another sabotaging effect of adapting yourself to wrest love from others. When we do this, we are occluding the beauty inherent in the body of Christ. In other words, when we try to be like others, we are not functioning as the part of the body He made us to be. We water down the witness of a colorful, diverse conglomeration of varying body parts by hiding who we truly are for the sake of some fleeting human acceptance. It would be like looking at a rainbow that has only a couple of colors in it. His body is made up of different parts. Each part is necessary for what He made it to be in order for the whole body to function well. This is clear in first Corinthians twelve. When we try to make the metaphorical hand function like a liver, it compromises the health of the whole body! Revising ourselves for others' approval is not only the wrong motivation for change, it also mars the beautiful body of Christ God intended.

Who's your daddy?

The only way we can overcome being caught in this trap is to value the unvarying approval of God over the conditional approval of people. If we look to something else as all-important, it actually compromises our health. For instance, the human body functions brilliantly when given the right food, the best oxygen, sunlight, and exercise. However, while the body still functions when fed wrong food, exposed to contaminated air, and allowed to languish, it is significantly less healthy. It is the same with us. When we are focusing on the Lord Jesus' work for our sustenance, the living Word of God as our bread, and the life-giving work of His Spirit as our purpose, watch out! But when we are looking to fragile, worldly substitutes for our nourishment, it will be like eating lots of junk food. Tastes great for a little while, but doesn't last and leaves you a little queasy in the process. That's just what it's like when we work hard for others' stamps of approval on ourselves.

This plays out in our relationships, too. When you put your hope in people, they can sense it. It is then that others will begin to avoid or withdraw from you. Intuitively, they know they can't give what you really want – which is unconditional, unlimited, unwavering reaffirmation that you are special. How God yearns that we would look to Him for such comfort and definition. He gives it "more than we could ask or imagine!" (Ephesians 3:20). This God who longs to be gracious to you, rises to show you compassion, and delights over you with joy wants to be the only One from whom you get your identity (Isaiah 30:18, Zephaniah 3:17). He is jealous that we so easily give this right away, and rightfully so. We are His sheep; He created our inmost being, and made us His workmanship (Psalm 100:3, 139:13, Ephesians 2:10). Seeking significance, meaning, and value anywhere else is like me going up to a cow and asking it to be my everything. It's that ludicrous to seek true love, purpose, and importance outside of the Lord.

A graven actuality

Jesus was able, even though he was an actual human being like us, to endure the agony of the cross. Why? His eyes were focused squarely on His Father, in whose love He trusted.

Though humans all around Him hurled insults, mocked, and discounted Him, He never struggled with insecurity because He knew whose He was. As a Christ-follower, it is fruitless to look to anything else other than the Lord as the source of our significance and affirmation. When we do, we grieve the heart of God.

Jeremiah 2:13 shows us this truth. It says, "My people have committed two sins: they have forsaken me, the spring of living water, and have dug their own cisterns, broken cisterns that cannot hold water." A cistern is a tank, reservoir, or container. When we turn from God's constant provision of strength, life, and comfort for us and look to something else, we are forsaking Him. Not only are we sinning in the process of looking elsewhere but God for our identity, we sin when we try to *preserve* ill-gotten meaning. We will try to shove all manner of significance-getters into internal reservoirs. We'll hold onto money, relationships, prestige, friends, alcohol, jobs, hobbies, you name it, if it seems to give us a sense of being important. To do so is to dig our own cistern. It's like we unconsciously say, "Well, God, your valuing of me is nice and all, but I need more, so I'll just get it from this thing that has made me feel pretty good about me." Then we get caught up in maintaining that cistern – working harder, making more money, having more or tighter relationships, drinking more alcohol, spending more time on the hobby. God is pretty clear that this will never work. He says these "reservoirs for making me feel valuable" (cisterns) are broken.

Try it, if you don't believe it (although I really don't want you to). No amount of money, power, friendships, sex, possessions, positions – nothing will ever satisfy like we think. Look even now at the ways in which you seek meaning and feel value through something or someone in your life. Then ask God to show you what that is doing to your relationships. Honestly, your wife doesn't feel special because you have given all your affection to your fantasy football picks or your recent stock purchase. Your children might be acting out because your obsessive housecleaning has sent them the message that your belongings merit more time than they. Your long-time friend probably feels replaced by your "new and shiny" acquaintance who holds power in the community. Your old neighbors certainly will back off when they perceive how proud you are of your new larger home in the neighborhood with the best school system. The point is not to bash any one thing negatively, but to succinctly say that our relationships suffer when we are looking elsewhere but to God for significance.

Relationships suffer when we look to others rather than to God for significance.

In His Word, God tells us that springs of living water are to flow through us and will when we are firmly grounded on Him (John 7:38). When we look to Him for our identity and security, we give His Spirit dwelling within us greater space and freedom to work through us. In so doing, we have fresh energy. It's the manna concept or the daily bread principle. When the Lord is the focus of our lives as opposed to ourselves or some other pursuit, He gives us exactly what is needed for every day. We have a "spring" of fresh water when we give God preeminence in our lives.

On the flip side, when we seek self-definition outside of our Creator, we are attempting to hold purpose in some broken cistern. That is the opposite of springs of living water flowing through us. Moving water is healthy water, starting from a source and moving out to give nourishment far beyond that original source. That is the picture of us if we will refuse to dam up blessing in some cracked basin. However, if we do choose something other than God for our significance, we will be like a lake with standing water. What happens with water that does not move? It becomes a toxic breeding ground for all sorts of nastiness. This is the same for us. If we are looking elsewhere for affirmation of who we are, we are attempting to hold onto self-made buckets for feeling valuable. When we do this, we become toxic in some way – usually bitter, sometimes disillusioned, always insecure. No wonder it grieves the heart of a God who sent His Son for our freedom (Galatians 5:1). If you've wondered before why you are always so negative, perhaps you've just seen that it's because you don't really seek God to give you perspective and purpose, but instead look to the outside world.

At this point in our discussion, it's important to call a spade a spade. Hoarding value by finding our significance in others or things is idolatry. The cisterns we make are idols. Anything serving as a substitute for God that we turn to for meaning, value, and purpose is an idol. We tend to distance ourselves from thinking idolatry is a sin we commit because of our connotation of idols as golden calves and pot-bellied buddhas. However, anything can become an idol in our modern world. A relationship, our children, excellent grades, a good job, a luxury car, brand name purses, even our morning Starbucks – virtually anything can become a counterfeit for the comfort, identity, and affirmation of God. Such God-substitutes damage more than just us. As we see in the Old Testament, anytime idolatry is present, relationships are threatened, clear thinking is gone, and pervasive fretting abounds. What is your idol?

Roots and fruits

One way to determine if we have an idol in our lives is gleaned through the principles of John fifteen. Jesus said, "Remain in me, and I will remain in you. No branch can bear fruit by itself; it must remain in the vine. Neither can you bear fruit unless you remain in me. I am the vine, you are the branches" (John 15:4, 5). Christ's point to His disciples is that when we are planted in Him, we bear fruit. The principle extrapolated out is that the fruit tells much about the root. As you examine the fruit in your life, what you are rooted in becomes obvious.

For instance, if you are constantly disappointed in relationships, then your root is likely in the wrong place. You are probably founded on "my relationships with others will make me feel valuable and significant." If a fruit observed is pervasive discontentment, then you might be rooted in a false definition of happiness. Common results when we are rooted in some wrong cistern include: shame, overeating, overspending, depression, anxiety and panic, obsessive thoughts, compulsive behaviors, substance abuse, and excessive guilt. These show us that we are looking to someone or something else other than God for our significance. We could have anxiety because we are rooted in control – "If I can control enough things, then I will feel good about myself." We overspend because we believe accumulating more will bring us the satisfaction we long for – "If I can just get *that*, then I will be important or beautiful." We obsess because we are fixated on a certain earthly outcome which has become hugely important. All these things give us clues as to what the negative fruit in our lives might be revealing to us.

Idolatry can also be found in the ways we escape, anesthetize, numb, reward ourselves or "check out" of life.

Why? Because, again, the issue is *reliance*. If you can't go to bed at night without the television fix, ask yourself why. How about going without that morning coffee, afternoon Coke or happy hour drink? What does that reveal about your dependency? Do you escape through romance novels? Video games? Movies? Shopping? These all show us we are attempting to get comfort and life from places other than God. Most of these things aren't inherently bad at all. It's about dependency and definition. On what do I depend to feel worthy or important and how do I define myself? If Christ is truly our sufficiency as believers, what does dependency on these other things tell us? He's our Savior, our Lord, our life. Only when we live like He is will we see true freedom in our relationships.

The fruits of a life solely entrenched in Christ alone are recorded in Scripture (Galatians 5:22). If the truth of God is firmly planted in our hearts, then peace-filled, loving, joyful lives result. As well, our relationships will receive the benefit of us being more patient, long-suffering, understanding, kind, self-controlled people, just to name a few of the beneficial fruits that come from being rooted in Christ. The book of first John explains that if we walk in the light as He is in the light, we will have fellowship with one another (1 John 1:7). To walk in the light conveys walking in the ways of Jesus, who was self-sacrificial, kind, patient, compassionate, wise, understanding, and self-controlled, among other things. In other words, when we enter our daily lives rooted in Christ, we have deeper relationships with others. When we walk in the world, we do not have true connectedness with each other, but when we follow Jesus' footsteps, true soul bonds can happen.

So, in a book about relating beyond the surface, we must see that we will never be able to have the kind of relationships we long for until we can root out the things we are looking to for value rather than Christ. To level your gaze on something is to stare intently, using it as your focal point. Do you believe with all your heart that everything else pales in comparison to Him? Are you to the place yet where you realize that God's love and acceptance is the only true source of freedom and joy? Can you now see why living for the approval of others actually hurts, not helps, your relationships? Level the gaze of your heart on Christ alone and see your relationships with others become soul connections.

Chapter Twelve
LIVE WITH NO REGRETS

My friend Sandra, her husband of 24 years, and their two children left for their favorite vacation spot to meet family and celebrate his parents' anniversary. Within hours of arrival, her husband died a sudden and unexpected death in front of her and their two teenage kids. While theirs was a normal relationship with its foibles and familiar failings, they really did find a way to enjoy one another, embrace life fully, and keep the big picture. My friend's grief, while profound, is uncomplicated by regret. Can you and I anticipate the same if we lost our spouse...our child...our parent, neighbor, friend, sister? To end a book on relationships with the admonition to "live with no regrets" is referring to *relational* regrets. While you certainly can't change what you regret about circumstances or what other people have done to you, *you can live life to minimize relational regret.*

To further punctuate this point, at the writing of this page, Mike and I are sitting here stunned and grief-stricken upon his return from Children's Hospital. We are processing the news that a child in our congregation has an aggressive and rare form of cancer. Two days ago, they thought it was something wrong with her stomach. Today she underwent her first of enough chemo treatments to keep her in the hospital for a minimum of six months. Life truly can change in an instant. Two days ago, siblings probably argued, teens likely complained, and family members were possibly taken for granted. We all do it. But in moments like these, petty irritations, small disagreements, and judgmental agendas fade away as they are put in their rightful perspective as insignificant. Much data about this has been implicit in the foregoing chapters, but we shall close *Soul Connection* by narrowing in on what it will take to be a person who lives with no relational regrets.

Swallowing self

First, you won't regret *being a giving person*. To give without expecting in return is not only one of the most mature postures from which to live life, it is also one of the most liberating. Previously, we have talked about unconditional love and surrendering expecta-

> *You won't regret being a giving person.*

tions. Regret means "to feel sorry and sad about something previously done or said that now appears wrong, mistaken, or hurtful to others."[62] Certainly, we want to minimize the number of hurtful things we say or do to one another. But, we could also regret *withholding* ourselves from others. The plain fact, as offered by John Maxwell, is that "everyone is an influencer of other people. It doesn't matter who you are or what your occupation is."[63] Indeed, we are all very influential whether we choose to believe that or not. The question of regret concerns embracing that reality and using our influence for others' good.

Scripture tells us this: "Do not withhold good from those to whom it is due, when it is in your power to do it"

(Proverbs 3:27). God designed us after Himself and filled us with good things to give to others. He cautions us to be certain that we give good to others, because He knows our souls will suffer when we don't. I guarantee you won't regret sacrificing your time, energy, money, and preferences to bless others, because that is "faithfully administering God's grace in its various forms" (1 Peter 4:10). However, you could very well regret withholding affection, encouragement, admonition, kindness, grace, or regret just plain living life in some self-protective cocoon. How many funeral parlor "if onlys" could we avoid by giving what we have to give?

The person striving to live life with no regrets understands that we do good today because there are spiritual benefits to such a life in addition to an immeasurable sense of earthly joy. Luke 6:35 says, "But love your enemies, do good to them, and lend to them without expecting to get anything back." When Jesus says to expect nothing in return, He is reminding us we should not be motivated by worldly benefit, but we are given strength for today by the promise of future reward. As well, in Luke 14:12-14: "When you give a luncheon or dinner, do not invite your friends, your brothers or relatives, or your rich neighbors; if you do, they may invite you back and so you will repaid. But when you give a banquet, invite the poor, the crippled, the lame, the blind, and you will be blessed. Although they cannot repay you, you will be repaid at the resurrection of the righteous." Said plainly, *don't do good deeds for earthly advantage; but do them for spiritual, heavenly benefits.* We never know when, or to what degree, our earthly good deeds will produce strong spiritual blessings. Think again of Hebrews 13:2: "Do not forget to entertain strangers for by so doing some people have entertained angels without knowing it."

Finally, *living with no relational regrets means making the choice to die to yourself.* The way to love others is not through love of self. In order to really love God and others, we must die to self. For instance, as a parent, you know you have ample opportunities every day to choose self or your child. Parents who consistently chose self are the ones who never get over a child's sudden death. While every good parent feels he or she is falling short, ones that have sacrificed for their children understand there is no idyllic family and live with minimal regret. Similarly, after 19 years of marriage, I still can feel the "self versus him" choice every time Mike and I have a conversation. Just this afternoon in some back-and-forth texts, I knew I could bless Mike and yet still had to push my will over that "choose him not you" hill before I did. As well, when my good friend called and needed to talk, I had to deliberately stop multitasking to really hear her, and all the while I could hear self clamoring to rise up against my choice. No matter what type of relationship we are talking about, there is a clear opportunity to say "no" to that inevitable shard of self that doesn't want to surrender.

While I am absolutely not advocating you become a doormat without personal preference, opinion, or need, I do know that in the long run, following Jesus' sacrificial ways leads to richer, more personally fulfilling relationships. Therefore, *living with no relational regrets unquestionably means to return to a relationship ended or paused because of struggle.* Yes, the swallow-your-pride, forgive-because-He-commands-it kind of restoration. If you had a falling out three years ago with your sister, is it really okay that neither of you are talking today? Why have you and your favorite friend cooled off in getting your kids together since you had that disagreement over child-rearing? You completely enjoyed your college roommate, but haven't kept in touch because of something he said at your wedding. Why? When your long-time buddy suddenly left your company to go work for another, while it angered you, is it really worth losing the friendship forever? This does not mean putting yourself in danger, returning to a relationship with a wicked abuser, or sacrificing yourself at the whims of a power-hungry nonbeliever. Within the parameters of people who love the Lord and have loved you to some degree, to live with no regrets requires that we "make *every effort* to live in peace with all men" (Hebrews 12:14, italics mine).

Living with no relational regrets will result in soul-connecting relationships. We set ourselves up for such successful connections with others when:

- ≈ We look beyond.

- ≈ We are full of grace.

- ≈ We listen loud.

- ≈ We stand in.

- ≈ We refuse to judge.

- ≈ We are not shocked when we see issues in others.

- ≈ We assume the best.

- ≈ We know our own squishy areas and have grace when we encounter another's.

- ≈ We self-disclose.

- ≈ We take the risk to love big and encourage.

- ≈ We lean into differences.

- ≈ We risk.

- ≈ We are not thwarted by fear.

Why not take it easy?

Why live the way this book describes? Isn't it easier to live selfishly, choosing to be around people who are easy to get along with? And why work so hard at relationships? Shouldn't ones that are good be fairly simple? Would I really regret not going above and beyond to repair a relationship, taking the risk to share my feelings with close friends, and not forgiving someone who inflicted that massive wound on my life? As a matter of fact, if you are a Christian, then yes. Why exist in this world living the ways outlined here? A few answers to this question follow.

The most basic answer to this question is because the *true test of a disciple is faithfulness*. Why do that which is suggested here? Because you are a chosen, loved, specifically created disciple of God Himself, and He asks you to be faithful to Him. "If you love me, feed my sheep," says this God who gave His all to feed us (John 21:16, 17). "And he has given us this command: Whoever loves God must also love his brother" (1 John 4:21). Being faithful to God implies a love for His created ones beyond our own selfish interests (Philippians 2).

The early disciples "devoted themselves to the apostles' teaching and to the fellowship" (Acts 2:42). The word here for "fellowship" is the Greek word "koinonia" which is translated as communion, partnership, participation, and fellowship.[64] The implication of Biblical passages containing this word is that when we remain in fellowship with Christ and participate (koinonia) in God's will, we are able to treat others as Christ treats us. Discipleship involves devoting ourselves to fellowship, which involves sacrificing our selfish ways for the needs of fellow believers. When those who are unfamiliar with God's heart see this kind of love in action through His body of believers, they can become drawn to the one thing they have been searching for their whole lives: God's unconditional love! The early believer's pattern remains the same for us – *true disciples commit themselves to fellowship.*

The real test of discipleship is not so much a strong start as ongoing faithfulness in that which matters to God. Having flashes of relational sacrifice or others-centeredness is wonderful. However, the signature of an earnest believer is a life dedicated to living out Christ's ways over the long haul. An apt

Christ followers don't love only when it's convenient.

picture for this mark of a disciple is Proverbs 17:17: "A friend loves at all times and a brother is born for adversity." *Christ-followers don't love only when it is convenient, but consistently over time.* Transformation will come as we do what is suggested in this book over time. Aristotle said, "We are what we repeatedly do. Excellence then is not an act but a habit."[65] If loving at all times is your learned habit, you will live with only a modicum of regret for your side of a relationship.

Another answer to the question of "why live this way?" is that others will be drawn to Jesus when we do. As the old song says, "they will know we are Christians by our love."[66] A life of true soul-connectedness is a beacon in our world of increasing technological and physical isolation. People who are lovingly unafraid to put themselves out there are amazingly refreshing. Aren't you intrigued by the stranger who will actually make eye contact or the person who chooses to talk to you about a tough subject in person rather then through the mask of email? Faithful people, grounded people, giving people, and loving people are magnetic. To live in the ways this book encourages through Scriptural insight is to in actuality live evangelistically. It takes one important understanding, though: *You have something to offer rather than something to prove.* When we finally realize this, Jesus' life becomes much more visible through our own. Then, amazingly when we live within this framework, we see the Christ who came to "proclaim release to the captives, and recovery of sight to the blind, to set free those who are downtrodden" doing those miracles *through us*! (Luke 4:18)

A final answer to "why live this way" returns us to our starting point in the introduction: *Because connection in deep places of the soul is God's idea and meant for us all.* Ecclesiastes advises us that "it is better to go to a house of mourning than to go to a house of feasting," "sorrow is better than laughter," and "the heart of the wise is in the house of mourning, but the heart of fools is in the house of pleasure" (7:2-4). The deeper, authentic times of life are richer than the fleeting, funny ones. Both are wonderful, but intimacy comes through a soul exposed and met with love. People get closer through one tragedy than through years of prosperity.

So really then, why do we evade, cover, hide, and distance ourselves when we know in our deepest heart that we long for closeness and connection? Every person on the face of the earth longs to be deeply known and unconditionally loved and accepted for who they are. Any connection that takes us to that is God's idea and a vessel through which His life can flow more abundantly. Such is true intimacy. Dallas Willard beautifully captures this truth and exposes how our society has confused actual intimacy with sexual relationship:

"Intimacy is the mutual mingling of souls who are taking each other into themselves to ever increasing depths...The profound misunderstandings of the erotic that prevail today actually represent the inability of humanity in its current Western edition to give itself to others and receive them in abiding faithfulness. Personal relationship has been emptied out to the point where intimacy is impossible...

Yet intimacy is a spiritual hunger of the human soul, and we cannot escape it. This has always been true and remains true today. We now keep hammering the sex button in the hope that a little intimacy might finally dribble out. In vain. *For intimacy comes only within the framework of an individualized faithfulness within the kingdom of God."*[67] (italics mine)

Willard effectively brings us back to faithfulness to God. We can't escape our desire to be truly connected to others, but this will not happen unless our lives are first dedicated to God and to being faithful to His ways - which include the self-sacrificial, unconditionally loving guidelines in this book.

All the way in

In our society of short attention spans and instant everything, I am really impressed by the fact that you are still reading. Bless you for wanting all that God wants through your life. I'm sincerely asking the Lord that you sense His closeness and pleasure as you faithfully complete the reading of this work. Because He uses all things for His purposes, you are now at a decision point. I pray that you "see to it that you do not reject the One who speaks" (Hebrews 12:25) and by faith believe Him for true and lasting change.

Awhile back, Mike and I attended the U.S. Open tennis tournament in New York. We landed ourselves on an express train the first time we traveled to the Open from our hotel. It was a different time of day when we tried to find that same train again, so we got on one going the same route, but we were unable to tell if it was an express or not. As people crowded in and the wait extended, we asked a young Italian-looking man wearing an ill-fitting suit if this was the express. He glanced over his left shoulder, then his right, and shrugged. In the thickest New York accent you can imagine, he said, "I dunno. It iz whad it iz. Ya git there evenshully."

A decision point for you at the close of this book is if you will believe that doing even some of these godly principles will get you there eventually. It really "is what it is" – you get out of relationships what you put in them. Can you by faith agree with God that His ways are best and worth whatever effort is necessary? In so doing, as you make small changes and practice relational concepts recorded in these pages, you will reap the benefit of true life-giving, soul-connecting relationships. However, you have to believe that doing something is better than doing nothing and refuse to be overwhelmed at the magnitude of all the complexity that relationships contain. Instead, commit yourself to small efforts and believe that they will "pay off."

As we continued on our New York ride, we discovered that no trains were express during that time of day. This reality played out as we stopped at station after station and more and more people crowded on. At each station, the engineer would have to ask people to move into the train all the way so that the doors might close. Literally, stop after stop, the begging operator would not be able to start moving until the doors could shut. Doors don't shut with people in them, so he would over and over remind people to move the entire way into the train or it couldn't go. As if monitored by a higher-up, he said politely every time, "Awl the way in the train...puleez." The "please" was breathy, low, and full of air, as if a routine and insincere afterthought which practically fell off the sentence.

We didn't know if it was our imagination or not, but he seemed to become a little more exasperated with each loudspeaker petition to move in. Finally, at one stop, he decided it was time for a lecture in classic New York fashion. With thick accent, he said, "We have a lot of people trying to get to the Open. We have a lot of people trying to get to Man-aa-nn (Manhattan). Youns have to stick yahselves awl the way in the train...puleez." Did he really say "stick yourselves" in the train, we wondered?! We began to giggle at *sticking* yourself in, as opposed to moving in or pushing in towards the center of the train. Sure enough, he said, "...stick yourselves all the way in."

What a great concept for us! The message to "stick yourselves all the way in" is that you're not going to get where you want to go unless you put yourself all the way in – clear to the center; not one foot in, one foot out. For our relationships to be fulfilling, rewarding, and amazing, we must be "all in" with them, as the poker player. We can't hold back, play timid, or bluff our way to good relationships. However, if we thrust ourselves into the merciful hands of a gracious God, we can then truly invest ourselves for the hope of quality relationships that bless His heart.

We can stick ourselves all the way into our relationships, rather than tiptoeing around, trying to play it safe.

Why? Because we follow a God who stuck Himself all the way in to a degree we cannot imagine. As Christ was pierced for our transgressions, His life now frees us to willfully place ourselves in deep. He is our strength. He is our confidence. He is our guide. He is our barometer for how things are going, not others. He is our feedback for how we are doing. He is the one who invites us to expect lots from Himself, while lessening our hopes in other people. He is our example. He is our comforter. He is our best friend. We can stop living in relationally immature fear-based ways because of Him.

So, will you be a shallow or deep person? Shallow people live hoping that there won't ever be any conflict, challenge, or struggles. Deep people know that true community is messy. Relationships by their very *definition* are messy. Shallow people try to shut out the bad. Deep people allow for it all, knowing that when you live life trying to shut out the bad, you also shut out the good and end up with a very limited range of expression and experience. The shallow person allows the conversation to be about things, events, and others. The deep person asks, "What do we *really* want to be talking about?" and leads the conversation to feelings, fears, Christ, hopes, dreams, faith, and honest expressions. My deep friend this morning emailed me and quoted a phrase I once said of myself, repeating it back for herself. She said, "I just don't deal well in shadows." She continued with what I see as a true indicator of a person of depth: "I long for authentic community and know it is possible in Jesus." No matter how old you are, it's time to decide: Are you going to continue to contribute to the shallow functioning that this world peddles or are you going to relate beyond the surface?

Years ago, Mike and I had a small group that couldn't have been more motley-crew-esque. There was a Ph.D. college professor, a marijuana-smoking welder, an overly-Southern Mary Kay consultant, a feisty Italian fighter pilot, his stunning Barbie-doll wife, the white social worker mother of three adopted African-American crack babies, a twice-divorced passive middle-aged desk jockey, an Assembly of God holy roller, a La Leche league leader, and us, newly-married and wide-eyed. Unbeknownst to me at the time, God was using that group to cement in my soul seeds of a template for true relating that have since informed years of ministry and even this book. We chose a light study – Larry Crabb's *Inside Out*. Of course, I'm being facetious. That book is anything but light. What God did through it, though, was to draw out a level of authenticity by His Spirit that stirred everyone's soul. We prayed together; we shared vulnerable things; we experienced confrontation and even outright fighting, but somehow we all knew we were safe. Initial judgments between members melted away as God's Word pierced us, and each other's true souls emerged. I'll never forget Jack (the welder), with fire in his eyes confronting Harry (the professor). He said, "I don't care what you say. That's not what you really think." And from there, a huge and ongoing discussion ensued about why Christians become veiled "I-have-it-all-together" people.

It was only in subsequent years and multiple small groups later that I realized how rare such a group was. Most people won't even think of going deep, admitting failure, owning insecurity, needing help holding onto faith, being fueled by hope, and loving without regard for self in a group of any size. But what occurred in that group was transcendence beyond the ordinary to the depth of the soul. It was evidenced by a level of group attendance, punctuality, engagement, and completion of homework that just doesn't happen. That their appetites were whet for true community was proven by consistent attendance. For years after, the members of that group recalled those moments together as the time of greatest spiritual development in their lives.

What happened for those people was something captured in words by a friend of mine recently. He said, "Sometimes our biggest desire is just to know and be known. Just to have someone walk beside you." There is an unconscious loneliness lifted when someone else knows our story and carries our thoughts with us, even if just a little. A client of mine said to me last week of her struggle with friends, "I just like it when I have good, soul conversations. They're real. What better than to share personal struggles, preferences, and ideas?" But she finds few others who are willing to put themselves "out there" like her. Again, a question for us all is: will we be shallow or deep? Not just in our conversation, but in the level of peace within our own soul. Will joy that is a by-product of a sustained focus on the Lord be a true characteristic of ours? The only way we can hope to be fearless enough to live boldly, unhindered, and sacrificially in relationship is by placing our hope in Him, and not in people. It is by aligning our behavior and lives with the Word of God rather than our personal proclivities, preferences, and understandings.

A higher plane

We started this book with the truth that we were made for relationship. No man is an island, indeed. To be human is to long for relationships with other humans. We weren't made for shallow paddling about, but for swimming through all types of water. We were created to exchange – to exchange life with others. To allow the life of Christ within us to impact and intermingle with others and vice versa. Do you remember the people at the beginning of this book whose initials you wrote down? Think again of the person with whom you have the worst relationship presently. Which of the chapters is most pertinent to that relationship? What shifts do you need to make in your thinking or behavior? How does God view this person, you, and the relationship between the two of you? What will you do differently in that relationship because God has been speaking throughout the pages of this work? What is even just one principle you can take and apply with that person?

Every day in this world we will be bombarded with messages encouraging us to demand our rights, look out for number one, and smugly distance ourselves when we disagree with others. Jesus, however, has told us to follow His example and choose love instead. And Jesus' love does not seek personal justice. This is why He told His disciples that if someone took their coats, they should give him their shirts as well (Matthew 5:40). Christ's example shows us that true love will give up its rights. Why? "Because love lives on a higher plane."[68] Love in the higher plane will live where others can take advantage of you. But no matter what anyone else does to you, you can always choose love. This love that follows Jesus' example isn't a "mushy feeling; it's a compelling force, a deliberate choice to be guided by God in the practical, everyday encounters of life."[69] Such willfulness is what Jesus was talking about when He admonished us, "Whoever forces you to go one mile, go with him two" (Matthew 5:41). Mature love goes beyond what is required. Love lives on a higher plane.

Norman Cousins said, "Death is not the greatest loss in life. The greatest loss is what dies inside us while we live."[70] What hope has been thwarted in you that God is calling out to come alive again? How has self-protection in some form become "ops normal" for you such that you will know peace and freedom when it is gone? Is there a death in others that you can breathe life into by your willingness to love big, be safe, really listen, or boldly question another? This God who gave us life is constantly speaking life to us and drawing us to be life-givers to others. If true soul connection in this manner is your heart's desire and your faith is placed squarely on Him, watch how He blesses people through you and you through others.

You have been given a toolbox with tools for God-honoring relationships. As you pull out each one and familiarize yourself with it, believe God for that which has previously been missing in your relationships. Expect that He will bless your attempts, and though overnight change will not occur, continued usage of these tools over the long haul will transform both you and your relationships. Remember it is His glory that is the ultimate outcome of such endeavoring. "Faith expects from God what is beyond all expectation."[71] Of your desire for true soul connection, I pray yours is the faith that expects more from God than you ever thought possible. By faith, move forward, no – run like the wind! – toward all God intends for you and your relationships on this earth.

Appendix One
FACILITATING GROUP "SOUL CONNECTIONS"

The concept of "soul connection" in a group format actually arose and has evolved from a group exercise I started doing years ago. Primarily in youth ministry at the time, I would have students grab questions from a hat, we'd pray that God would move and speak, and some deep sharing would commence. This format morphed and grew over the years into a deep time of intentional and focused sharing from the heart while attempting to follow the movement of the Holy Spirit. I carried it with me through my doctoral program, into my role as a pastor's wife, and then nationally with ministry leadership training. Somewhere along the line, one leader who asked me to facilitate the group called it "soul connection," and it has stuck ever since.

No matter whether it is a group of eclectic scholars, tattooed students, or earnest youth ministers-in-training, the outcome of soul connection is nearly the same every time. Hearts are touched, bonds are developed, tears are shed, and God is glorified through the honest, loving interactions of His children. At the moment we shed self-protective ways, we simultaneously mature. It has been a fascinating journey to watch people talk about what is really happening in their souls. When it comes to issues of the heart, we're all fundamentally the same. Longings, confessions, and fears are similar. Perceptions of God, issues of performance, and overconcern with peers are predominant regardless of age or stage of life. When the framework is set for authentic sharing to take place, people drink it in like kittens tasting their first milk. When someone realizes that we are all basically alike in our wishes, hurts, dreams, desires, insecurities, worries, and wants, that moment is huge. Typical defensiveness seems to melt in the face of true vulnerability.

From a camp deep in the hills of Western Pennsylvania to universities in San Francisco to missions in Amsterdam, I've personally witnessed the power that these group soul connections can have. Whether with students at large universities, children raised in Ukraine, middle-aged soccer moms, successful businessmen, or immature adolescents – it doesn't matter. While the players and variables can be drastically different, the outcome is the same. Why are these so successful? It is because when done right, our deepest longing to be known and loved is joined with a prerequisite for such relationships – acceptance. The commitment to expressing kindness, to being safe people, and to being open and non-judgmental means that every word, every tear is met with acceptance and gratitude for the sharing.

I believe the reason these soul connections are so successful has to do with setting expectations. First, we set the anticipation that God is working in each of our hearts, and wants to do so through this exercise. So, whatever question a person receives, he is asked to see that as ordained by God specifically for him (rather than wishing for the question someone else gets). Second, we set expectations for how to behave to best facilitate an open and safe environment. Third, ask everyone to believe that these are going to be times where we are settling in long enough to "be still and know that he is God" in a group setting (Psalm 46:10).

The guidelines for promoting a safe and open discussion have included the following:

1. A person can share to whatever level he or she wants. All disclosures are met with acceptance and appreciation.

2. The truism "you get out of something what you put into it" is offered as a reminder to use this situation to get all God wants for a person out of it.

3. Everything is confidential and kept in the group setting.

4. For additional safety, no one is permitted to bring up to another person something that person shared in the group time unless he or she begins talking about it first. So, even if I have questions about Wendy's comment and really want to ask her about it, I cannot unless she brings it up first.

5. While humor is a wonderful thing, soul connection is not a good time for it. Why? Because humor sabotages safety (especially sarcasm) and many people use humor as a mask to hide behind.

6. Everyone agrees to tune in and listen very hard for what others are saying, rather than simply waiting in anticipation for his or her turn.

7. Follow-up to a person's answer cannot happen except through the facilitator. So, if a person really wanted to ask a follow-up question, he or she would need to ask the facilitator first. The facilitator might then ask the person, "So-and-so has a follow-up question to your answer. Would you like to hear it or prefer not to? Either answer is just fine." For obvious reasons, the facilitator must be a person of discernment, wisdom, and grace.

The facilitator can open a group with a question intended for everyone to answer, such as :

1. Knowing that at some point or another, everyone puts up shields to try to keep people from seeing what's going on inside them, what mask do you wear?

2. What general sin area plagues you the most?

3. How do you personally mostly hear from the Lord?

4. On a scale of 1 – 10, how in sync do you sense you are with the Lord right now? (Ten being the best it's ever been, one being the worst).

5. Name the one time period in your life that you were the happiest and the one that you wish you could do over.

6. Is it more important for you to be appreciated, understood, accepted, or respected?

The goal with questions such as these is to quickly get people on board with the fact that everyone will be sharing. As well, the precedent is set that questions will be probing in nature, and designed to get people to discuss what doesn't come up in everyday conversation. So, actually going around the circle works here, even though suddenly switching it to the other end of the room is helpful in a larger group.

After getting everyone to agree to the guidelines and beginning with some "everyone answers" questions, it works well for the facilitator to begin giving individualized questions to different people. He or she is attempting to allow the Holy Spirit to direct questions spontaneously and randomly instead of going around in a circle. It is often best to choose people who can more easily express themselves in words or who are leaders in the group to get the early questions.

During this individualized question time, the facilitator can stop and have others speak to a person, especially one who is bound in lies or who has made a significant disclosure. For instance, when John shares that he just doesn't feel like others value him, the facilitator could ask him to name someone in the group whom he admires. If he answers, "Sarah," then the facilitator could direct Sarah to give John some feedback about what impact he has had on her. Perhaps Ashley discloses that she is depressed, and feels like she will never be special to anyone. As this is clearly evidence of a hellish lie (because it's antithetical to God's truth), the facilitator could direct the entire group to encircle her and pray over her. If an individual shares something vulnerable, the facilitator can direct someone else to give an encouraging word, a hug, or a prayer. The facilitator can use the person with a mercy gift to go and comfort another. Such direction is best when utilized judiciously, as manipulating for attention could occur otherwise.

When the facilitator is asked what a question means, he or she does not interpret it for the person, but responds to the effect, "However you take it." The facilitator needs to be comfortable with long stretches of silence, keeping his or her eyes trained on the person answering. The facilitator is careful not to grace interruption or distraction with a response. In other words, if someone across the room cracks a joke during another's answer, the facilitator's gaze does not leave the person answering. Such subtleties help set a positive, respectful, expectant tone. Here are some questions of the type that the Holy Spirit might lead a facilitator to ask:

1. What's the last special touch or time or word from the Lord you've had?

2. Who do you really want to tell you that they are proud of you?

3. Do you have many secrets or a few?

4. What's one question you'd never want anyone to ask?

5. What is one thing God has shown you about Himself this past year?

6. How are you different as a person than you were a year ago?

7. What is one hope you have for the upcoming year?

8. What is a way you are being set free in the last five years?

9. When's the last time you cried?

10. What is one misconception of God that you have and what do you think has caused that (relationship with father/mother/sibling, a trial, a hurt, wrong teaching)?

11. What brings you the most joy?

12. When do you find you feel the closest to the Lord?

13. What do you look forward to?

14. What is something the Lord has asked you to surrender?

15. Do you tend to have too high of expectations of people or too low?

16. Who is a role model of yours?

17. What would you say is the most significant shaping experience of your life (one that has formed a large part of who you are)?

18. Do you have a lot of little fears or few big ones?

19. Do you tend to be a glass-half-empty or a glass-half-full person?

20. If you could have any superpower, what would it be, and why?

21. When you are going about your day, what do you think about most of the time?

22. How would you want a friend to describe you?

23. I want to be more _____ and less _____.

24. What do you struggle with in rank order from most to least: personality, spirituality, sexuality?

25. How do you see God in rank order from most to least: King, Friend, or Father?

26. When was the last time you felt loved?

27. Have you been happy with who you've been? Why or why not?

28. Which one is the hardest for you:

   ➢ Experiencing forgiveness when you mess up?

   ➢ Being humbled and broken before God?

   ➢ Thanking God for who you are and how He's made you?

   ➢ Seeing God in everyday circumstances?

29. What is a regret you have? What is a time of great joy?

30. What makes you feel more loved than anything else and when is the last time it's happened?

31. What is an area God is refining in you in the past year?

32. If others could have a clear view of what's really in your heart – if the layers were peeled back, what would they see?

33. What is your greatest sense of accomplishment?

34. Who is someone whose approval you try to get more than anyone else's?

35. What is something God has asked you to do that you are not doing now?

Also, if this is a group that knows each other well or is meeting for a specific length of time or purpose, asking about group dynamics is always fruitful. Here are some questions to that end:

1. How do you think you've come across to the group and how do you think they perceive you?

2. Do you owe someone in this group an apology?

3. Are there pockets/cliques in this group?

4. How vulnerable and open have you been to these people?

5. Who do you think is the most similar to you and the most different from you in this group?

6. How real do you think you have been with these people on a scale of 1 to 10, 10 being completely, totally open and 1 being as closed as possible?

Finally, it is often quite moving to have the entire group spend time encouraging one another. The best way to do this is to say, "What do we like about so and so?" and have others give their feelings. The facilitator also needs to be prepared to offer encouraging words to every person. This actually takes quite a bit of time, depending on the size of the group, so it is not best to do so when there's not much time left. That will leave some feeling unimportant, left out, or even hurt that they didn't get time for being appreciated. In general, if your desire is for God to be glorified by a group you are in, fostering soul connection times such as these can help you. Our Lord is gracious to honor earnest effort towards love and good deeds, not to mention unity (Hebrews 10:24-25, Ephesians 4:3, Romans 15:5, Hebrews 12:14).

Appendix Two
MANAGING CONFLICT IN A CHRIST-LIKE WAY

Conflict can be an unwelcome gift. While no one enjoys it, and few can manage the emotions surrounding it, if two people can make it through a disagreement, their relationship will often be better as a result. Because of this, the way a conflict is resolved is often more important than the resolution itself. If conflict is badly handled, one of the parties can suffer wounds that are difficult to heal. Instead, if certain parameters and perspectives are kept, both parties can benefit and even become more godly in the process. When you find yourself needing to negotiate a challenging space with another, the following commitments will help:

1. Realize that no disagreement is enough to end a relationship forever. No matter how serious it might be, no issue is worth destroying a friendship, partnership, or family tie. (1 Peter 4:8)

2. Commit to viewing each other through Christ's eyes, unconditionally. (2 Corinthians 5:16-18)

3. Each person needs to agree to honesty and acceptance. (Romans 15:7)

4. For an issue to be resolved, both parties must agree to seek to understand each other. This is accomplished by listening to each other's feelings, even if they seem inappropriate to you. (James 1:19)

5. Each person agrees to assume 100% of the responsibility for resolving the conflict. The 50/50 idea doesn't work to bring total resolution. (Romans 14:19)

6. The conflict needs to be limited to the here and now. Bringing up past failures shows only that you are living in unforgiveness. The discussion needs to be limited to the one issue that is the center of the disagreement. (Colossians 3:13)

7. These phrases will shut down the conversation:

    "You never..." (The truth is "You rarely...")

    "You always..." (The truth is "You often...")

    "I can't... " (The truth is "I won't...")

    "I'll try..." (The truth is "I'll make a half-hearted effort...")

    "You should..." or "You shouldn't..." (These are shame-based statements.) (Proverbs 22:11)

8. Focus must be on the issue at hand rather the character or personhood of the other. (Ephesians 4:2)

9. Both parties need to use "I feel..." statements. This keeps the focus off of blame. (Ephesians 4:15)

10. Look for the way in which God might be using this person, this situation, and even this issue as an instrument of His, working in your life. (Rom. 8:28)

11. Because each person will ultimately answer to the Lord, never counterattack, even if the other person does. (Ephesians 4:26)

12. Parties must stick to sharing how they feel about what has occurred, not ascribe motives to the other. (Ephesians 4:31)

13. When someone is not clear about what is being said, he or she asks for clarification. (Proverbs 2:11)

14. While it is fine for parties to be honest about their emotions, they must keep them under control. (Proverbs 15:18)

15. It is important that both individuals keep in the forefront that the resolution of the conflict is what is important, not whether one wins or loses. If the conflict is resolved, both parties benefit. Believers are on the same team, not opposing ones. (Ephesians 4:25)

16. Each party needs to agree ahead of time what topics are out of bounds because they are too hurtful or have already been discussed (bad habits, obsessive hobbies, physical traits, etc.). (Proverbs 18:21)

17. Parties need to commit to praying before and after resolution discussions. (Philippians 4:6)

18. Finally, each again must consider whether this conflict is something that can be overlooked and forgiven or if it truly merits the effort of resolution. (Proverbs 19:11)

Adapted from *Worry-Free Living* by Frank Minirth, Paul Meier, and Don Hawkins. (Nashville: Thomas Nelson, 1991). Another fantastic resource is *The Peacemaker* by Ken Sande. (Grand Rapids, MI: Baker Books, 2004).

Appendix Three
SOUL CONNECTING WITH ADOLESCENTS

An entire book could be written on how to capture and connect with the heart of a teen. What complexities lie beneath these beings! However, to truly love a teen or pre-teen is not impossible. Offered here are just a few reminders of who these morphing people are and how to break through the communication barrier. By no means is this intended to be an exhaustive exposition, just a little helping hand.

1. Don't forget they live in the moment. You'll never connect with them if you don't remember that they won't have the longer-term, wider-angle perspective that you do.

2. If you minimize their "moment," you will lose all hope of connection. (Okay, perhaps I'm exaggerating a bit, but it seems befitting the subject at hand – adolescents.)

3. They need to hear truth from the adults in their lives.

4. While they're not 3rd graders anymore, they're also not adults. That means that sometimes they act mature and other times, like babies. We can't anticipate which they're going to appear to be from one moment to the next.

5. They are in process. There's something much, much deeper than we can see that is happening inside them.

6. Teens can spot a fake immediately.

7. Adolescents respond to someone who is consistent and genuine over someone who is cool and edgy.

8. Their hormones are raging. You must simply write off some of their maddening machinations to this fact.

Helpful hints to connect with the heart of a teen:

1. <u>Take yourself back to those emotional roller coaster days of your own adolescence.</u> Remember the intense desire to fit in while feeling as though you stuck out? Recall being expected to act like an adult while being treated like a child? Think back to how much you wanted independence, and yet still wanted your parents to be parents. *This is empathy. Review chapter 6.*

2. <u>Whatever you do, don't minimize what they are going through.</u> Validate their "moment." A major blunder we can commit if our hope is true soul connection is to trivialize their struggles. It is easy to forget the pain we experienced during the same time in our lives. *This is compassion. Review chapter 1.*

3. A major task of adolescence is confirming identity. <u>Mirror to them their core qualities and characteristics</u> and they will be connected to you through their insecurity. This is blessing through speech. *Review chapter 8.*

4. <u>Encourage them and appropriately hug them no matter how they appear on the outside</u> (disinterested, tough, overconfident, apathetic, etc.) *This is looking beyond. Review chapter 1.*

5. <u>Listen, listen, listen</u>. Listen as much as you can. Don't pepper them with questions. Mostly, listen for the feelings behind the words. *Review chapter 3.*

6. <u>Accept them where they are</u>, trusting that God is still on the scene, involved, and working in their lives, according to His truth in Philippians 1:6. *This is acceptance. Review chapter 6.*

7. <u>Model honest communication yourself</u>. Be humble enough to admit mistakes, own wrongdoing, and acknowledge shortcomings. *This is humility. Review Jesus' entire life (and chapter 1).*

8. <u>Learn whatever you can about their world</u> – language, fads, school environment, etc. Know who their friends are and be near the action whenever possible. Learn what a teen's love language is and intentionally try to connect with him or her in this way. *This is wisdom. Review chapter 8.*

9. <u>Try to recognize whenever the adolescents in your life are falling prey to hellish lies about themselves, others, or God.</u> The teen years are critical times and if lies become their paradigm at this young age, it is often very challenging to correct that misperception with God's truth later in life. There is a reason that we can vividly recall hurtful times in middle and high school. It is because they have such deep impact on the development of our soul, character, and personality. Be willing to share God's truth, which presumes that you yourself are a continual student of the Word. *This is speaking the truth in love. Read <u>Soul Healing</u>, <u>Victory Over Darkness</u> (Neil Anderson), <u>Waking the Dead</u> (John Eldredge), Revelation 12:11.*

NOTES

1. Heller, Sharon, *The Vital Touch* (New York: Henry Holt and Company, LLC, 1997); De Angelis, Barbara, *What Women Want Men to Know* (New York: Hyperion, 2001), pp. 274-275; Mary Shivanandan, *Nurturing as Basic Right and Responsibility*, February, 2003. http://www.christendom-awake.org/pages/mshivana/nurture.html (accessed November 11, 2007); Goleman, Daniel. "The Experience of Touch: Research Points to a Critical New Role," *New York Times*, February 2, 1988.

2. Crabb, Larry and Dan Allender. *Hope When You're Hurting* (Grand Rapids: Zondervan, 1997), p. 182.

3. NASV stands for the "New American Standard" version of the Bible.

4. Crabb, Larry and Dan Allender. *Hope When You're Hurting* (Grand Rapids: Zondervan, 1997), p. 182.

5. John 8:1-11, adulteress; John 4: 1-26, Samaritan; Luke 8: 43-48, woman with issue of blood; Luke 19:1-10, Zaccheus; John 12:3, costly perfume

6. David Guzik, "Study Guide for John 12." *Blue Letter Bible,* July, 2006. http://www.blueletterbible.org/ (accessed October 10, 2007).

7. *Encarta Online Encyclopedia*, "Administer". Microsoft, 2003. http://encarta.msn.com/ (accessed November 24, 2007).

8. While its origin is unclear, many theologians and Christians explain the concept of grace with the acronym of "God's riches at Christ's expense." Hal Lindsey, John McArthur and others comment on the fuller meaning of this phrase.

9. Boltz, Ray and Steve Millikan, "Shepherd Boy," *Thank You,* Nashville: Shepherd Boy MusicASCAP, 1988.

10. Zaidel D. W., Aarde S. M., and Baig, K. "Appearance of symmetry, beauty, and health in human faces", *Brain and Cognition*, 57 no. 3 (2005). http://cogprints.org/4349/1/Zaidel2005.pdf (accessed January 10, 2008); Liu, Y. and Palmer, J. "A Quantified Study of Facial Asymmetry in 3D Faces," in *2003 International Conference of Computer Vision Proceedings of the 2003 IEEE International Workshop on Analysis and Modeling of Faces and Gestures, Carnegie Mellon Robotics Institute*. October, 2003.

11. Review Matthew 26:31-35, 69-75 for background on Peter.

12. Nahum 2:2, Acts 1:6

13. I believe he shared this sentiment at a conference in San Antonio, Texas, at MacArthur Park Church of Christ in the 1990s. Larry Crabb's website is www.newwayministries.org.

14. Chambers, Oswald, *My Utmost for His Highest* (New York: Dodd, Mead, and Company, 1963), May 3rd reading.

15. Wangerin, Walt. *As for Me and My House* (Nashville: Thomas Nelson, 1990).

16. Twain, Mark. http://www.allmarktwainquotes.com/ (accessed January 12, 2008).

17. Holter, Eric. "Reinvigorating the Christian Ministry of Exhortation." *Consider Christ*, February 4, 2006 http://consideringchrist.org/ (accessed January 18, 2008).

18. Holkeboer, Kathleen S. *"Are You a Courage Giver?"* Discipleship Journal, Issue 113, 1999.

19. Landorf Heatherly, Joyce. *Balcony People* (Georgetown, Texas: Balcony Publishing, 2004).

20. Silvious, Jan. *Big Girls Don't Whine* (Nashville: W. Publishing Group, a division of Thomas Nelson, Inc., 2003).

21. *Wikipedia: The Free Encyclopedia*, "Emotional Intelligence." http://en.wikipedia.org/ (accessed September 13, 2007).

22. Freedman, Joshua. *At the Heart of Leadership* (San Mateo: Six Seconds, 2007), p. 81.

23. *Queendom: The Land of Tests.* "Emotional IQ Test." http://www.queendom.com/tests/ (accessed December 8, 2007); Goleman, Daniel. *Emotional Intelligence* (New York: Bantam Books, 1995).

24. Carlson, Richard. *Don't Sweat the Small Stuff* (New York: Hyperion, 1997).

25. Musick, Dan. "Christ 'Emptied Himself' Philippians 2:7." *Kenosis*, 1997-2005. http://kenosis.info/index.shtml (accessed December 23, 2007).

26. Swindoll, Charles. *Grace Awakening* (Nashville: W. Publishing Group Div. of Thomas Nelson, 2003).

27. Crabb, Larry. *Inside Out.* (Colorado Springs: Navpress, 1988).

28. Carmichael, Amy. "Calvary Love," from *If,* (Fort Washington, PA: CLC Ministries, 1999).

29. Khosrow, Jahandarie. *Spoken and Written Discourse* (Connecticut: Praeger/Greenwood, 1999).

30. Tournier, Paul. <u>*Whole Person in a Broken World*</u> (New York: Harper & Row, 1964), p. 45.

31. Crabb, Larry and Dan Allender. *Hope When You're Hurting* (Grand Rapids: Zondervan, 1997), p. 196.

32. Crabb, Larry. *Inside Out* (Colorado Springs: Navpress, 1988).

33. Crabb, Larry. *Inside Out* (Colorado Springs: Navpress, 1988), p. 119.

34. Wright, H. Norman and Gary J. Oliver, *How to Change Your Spouse without Ruining Your Marriage.* (Ann Arbor: Vine, 1994).

35. Joshua 1:9, Galatians 5:1, Ephesians 6:13, 14,
2 Thessalonians 2:15

36. *The Free Dictionary*, "Litmus Test". http://www.thefreedic-tionary.com/ (accessed November 12, 2007).

37. Crabb, Larry. *Inside Out* (Colorado Springs: Navpress, 1988).

38. Maxwell, John. *Three-in-One Special Edition* (Nashville: Thomas Nelson, 2000).

39. Nouwen, Henri. *Turn My Mourning Into Dancing* (Nashville: W. Publishing Group, 2001), p. 26.

40. Jerry Maguire is an "R" rated movie, and so I would not give it a blanket recommendation. However, if you can get a cleaned-up copy, it is a great movie for examining multiple definitions and types of intimacy.

41. Sidney Jourard is a primary researcher on this topic, with his study from 1971 beginning a massive amount of further study on the topic; Derlega, Valerian J. and John H. Berg, *Self-disclosure: Theory, Research, and Therapy* (New York: Plenum Press, 1987).

42. Salinger, J. D., *The Catcher in the Rye* (Little Brown and Company, 1991), chapter 26.

43. Matthew 10:9-13, Mark 2:15-17

44. Henry, Matthew. *Matthew Henry Commentary on the Whole Bible*, (March, 1996). http://www.blueletterbible.org/Comm/mhc/ (accessed October 20, 2007).

45. Crabb, Larry. *Understanding People: Deep Longings for Relationship* (Grand Rapids, Michigan: Zondervan, 1987), p. 14.

46. Arthur, Kay. *Lord, I Give You This Day* (Colorado Springs, CO: Waterbrook Press, 2006), August 24th.

47. *Wikipedia: The Free Encyclopedia*, "Empathy." http://en.wikipedia.org/ (accessed May 30, 2007).

48. Piper, John. *Desiring God: Meditations of a Christian Hedonist* (Grand Rapids, Michigan: Multnomah, 2003), p.50.

49. *The Free Dictionary*, "Comparison." http://www.thefreedictionary.com (accessed October 27, 2007).

50. Merton, Robert K. *Social Theory and Social Structure* (New York: The Free Press, 1968).

51. This is an alternative translation for Proverbs 23:7 given in the NIV.

52. Gilligan, Stephen G. and Dvorah Simon. *Walking In Two Worlds: The Relational Self In Theory, Practice, And Community* (Phoenix, AZ: Zeig, Tucker & Theisen, 2004). Winance, Myriam. "How Speaking Shapes Person and World: Analysis of the Performativity of Discourse in the Field of Disability." *Social Theory & Health*, 5 (2007).

53. Wiley, Norbert. "The Self as Self-Fulfilling Prophecy." *Symbolic Interaction*. 26, no. 4 (2004). http://caliber.ucpress.net/doi/abs/10.1525/ (accessed January 18, 2007).

54. John Eldredge's *Waking the Dead* (2003) does an outstanding job of explaining spiritual agreements and the power they have over us if we are unaware. He also excellently explains how to reject hellish lies and walk in the freedom of Christ's truth.

55. Ferguson, Bill and Williams Ferguson. *Miracles Are Guaranteed* (Houston, TX: Return to the Heart, 2006).

56. Chapman, Gary. *The Five Love Languages* (Chicago: Northfield, 1995).

57. Wilson, Jim. "How to be Free From Bitterness." *The Free Grace Broadcaster*. http://www.mountzion.org/fgb/Summer03/FgbS5-03.html (accessed December 2, 2007).

58. Covey, Stephen. *Seven Habits of Highly Effective People* (New York: Fireside, 1989).

59. Gray, John. *Men are From Mars, Women are from Venus* (New York: HarperCollins, 1992).

60. Arthur, Kay. *Lord, I Give You This Day*. (Colorado Springs, Colorado: Waterbrook Press, 2006), September 15th.

61. Arthur, Kay. *Lord, I Give You This Day*. (Colorado Springs, Colorado: Waterbrook Press, 2006).

62. *Encarta Online Encyclopedia*, "Regret". Microsoft, 2003. http://encarta.msn.com/ (accessed November 28, 2007).

63. Maxwell, John and Jim Dornan. *Becoming A Person Of Influence (How To Positively Impact The Lives Of Others* (Nashville: Thomas Nelson, 1997).

64. *Blue Letter Bible*. "Lexicon search for fellowship." *Blue Letter Bible*, April, 2007. http://cf.blueletterbible.org/search/ (accessed January 16, 2008).

65. Aristotle, http://www.brainyquote.com/quotes (accessed January 22, 2008).

66. Scholtes, Peter. "They'll Know We Are Christians By Our Love." Los Angeles, CA: F.E.L. Publications, Ltd./ASCAP, 1966.

67. Willard, Dallas. *The Divine Conspiracy* (San Francisco: HarperCollins, 1998), p. 163.

68. Arthur, Kay. *Lord, I Give You This Day* (Colorado Springs, Colorado: Waterbrook Press, 2006), November 3rd.

69. Arthur, Kay. *Lord, I Give You This Day* (Colorado Springs, Colorado: Waterbrook Press, 2006), November 4th.

70. *Wikipedia: The Free Encyclopedia*, "Norman Cousins." http://en.wikipedia.org/ (accessed January 17, 2008).

71. Stamm, Millie. *Be Still and Know* (Grand Rapids, MI: Zondervan, 1978), p. 127.

Once you start *living beyond the pain of your past...*

...you can begin *relating beyond the surface!*

ORDER FORM

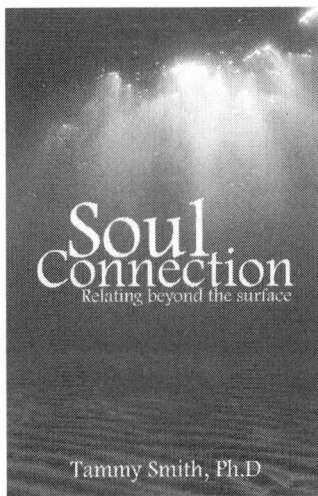

Please send me:

- ☐ Soul Healing: Living beyond the pain of your past
- ☐ Soul Healing Forever: Study Guide *(not pictured)*
- ☐ Soul Connection

Name: _____

Address: _____

City: _____ State: _____ Zip: _____

Phone: _____ Email: _____

Please include check or money order for $11.99 for each book or $15.00 for any two books, & mail to:

Threshold
1115 Bethel Road, Suite 204
Columbus, OH 43220

Free Shipping!

For more information or online orders, go to:

www.onthethreshold.org